EDITOR: Richard Morscheck.
BOOK DESIGN: Owen Neils.
COLOR SEPARATIONS: Modern Litho
    Corporation, Grand Rapids.
PRINTING: The John Henry Company, Lansing.
BINDING: John H. Dekker & Sons, Grand Rapids.
PAPER: 80-pound Signature Gloss by the
    Mead Corporation, Escanaba.
TYPE: Headlines set in Berling. Text set in 12
    point Paladium on the EditWriter 7500.

SPECIAL NOTE: Unless otherwise indicated in
the corresponding photo caption, all photographs,
illustrations, artifacts, and memorabilia are from
the private collection of the author, James Clary
of St. Clair, Michigan.

Library of Congress Catalog Number: 81-620035.
ISBN Number: 0-941912-01-9.

Ladies of the Lakes is Volume III of the Michigan
Heritage Series, and is a publication of
TwoPeninsula Press, a unit of

NATURAL RESOURCES MAGAZINE
Box 30034, Lansing, MI 48909

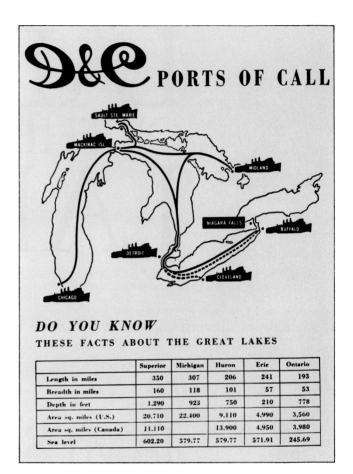

D&C PORTS OF CALL

DO YOU KNOW
THESE FACTS ABOUT THE GREAT LAKES

	Superior	Michigan	Huron	Erie	Ontario
Length in miles	350	307	206	241	193
Breadth in miles	160	118	101	57	53
Depth in feet	1,290	923	750	210	778
Area sq. miles (U.S.)	20,710	22,400	9,110	4,990	3,560
Area sq. miles (Canada)	11,110		13,900	4,950	3,980
Sea level	602.20	579.77	579.77	571.91	245.69

Editor's Preface

The five Great Lakes—Superior, Michigan, Huron, Erie, and Ontario collectively make up the largest body of fresh water in the world. With a combined surface acreage of 94,710 square miles, the lakes were gradually formed over a period of some 12,000 years of glacial activity which began nearly 15,000 years ago. That so large a body of fresh water evolved here, and that Michigan, in fact, is surrounded by four of the five Great Lakes, it is difficult to accurately measure the full meaning which these mighty waters have brought to the inhabitants of this state. In virtually every period of Michigan history, in addition to satisfying basic human needs for water, the lakes have played a prominent role in transportation, commerce, and recreation.

Therefore, it is appropriate for this book to re-create a part of that rich heritage which the Great Lakes and their connecting waters have bestowed upon us all. This book is a delightful and informative narrative of maritime history and you, the reader, are invited to join us on a pleasant excursion cruise, to participate in a great sea battle, to experience the terror of a ship disaster, and to come along for a ride aboard a giant freighter. *Ladies of the Lakes* is the third book in the *Michigan Heritage Series*, a collection of books about our state, its people and its natural resources. Volume I, *Visions of the Wild*, is a photographic tribute to the beauty of our state and the wonderful natural world in which we live. Volume II, *Mackinac, The Gathering Place*, is a celebration of the search for American historical roots being carried forward at the Straits of Mackinac. And Volume III, which you hold in your hands, is a salute to those schooners, steamers, gunboats, and freighters, those grand and glorious ships which make up our Great Lakes tradition and heritage.

One final note: No tax money was used to produce or publish this book, as well as the other books published in this series. All costs were paid by the *Michigan Natural Resources* fund which survives on subscriptions and book revenues only. All proceeds from the sale of this book will return to that fund to build the magazine and other future publications about our state. *Michigan Natural Resources Magazine* and Woolly Bear productions, its internal byproducts unit, is a working unit in the Michigan Department of Natural Resources.

Richard Morscheck

Richard Morscheck, Managing Editor
Michigan Natural Resources Magazine

THIS BOOK IS DEDICATED
TO ANN

Acknowledgements

I will be forever grateful to the many individuals and institutions that contributed to the research for my artwork and subsequent development of this book, *Ladies of the Lakes.* The late Robert E. Lee, former Director of the Dossin Great Lakes Museum, for his kind direction and support. Miss Janet Coe Sanborn, Editor of *Inland Seas,* for early guidance. Art O'Hara, Great Lakes Historical Society, for assistance in collecting data. Joseph Oldenburg, Burton Historical Collection, Detroit Public Library, for his help in researching. William Bates, Collector, for his time and direction. Harry Wolf, Photographer, for his interest and use of photographs. Mrs. Paul Allen Leidy, for providing information on the *David Dows.* John Levanen, Photographer, for encouragement and support. David Groover, Diver, for his contribution to the *David Dows* project. Dr. Robert Clifford, Collector, for his enthusiam and interest. Dr. Henry Gessel, for his support. The late Oswald Emig, for his fascinating stories of the *Tashmoo* and kind help. Patrick Labadie, Lake Superior Marine Museum, for his assistance. Frank Mays, for his time and contribution to the *Carl D. Bradley* project. John Horton, for his assistance on the *Cliffs Victory* project. Dr. Alexander C. Meakin, President, Great Lakes Historical Society, for use of photos. Harvey Nissley, Model builder, for his fine work on the *David Dows* and other models. Loudon Wilson, Historian, for his kind assistance.

There were many others who contributed time, provided information, photographs, and encouragement including William Hayward, Wilson Wonsey, Bill Browning, Ralph Browning, Gordon Bugbee,

Robert Batte, Jim McDonald, Rev. Peter Van Der Linden, Frank Crevier, Ted Richardson, Marjorie Ware, Milton Brown, Rev. Edward J. Dowling, Donald Reddeman, John Guba, Phil Mason, Harry Carle, Harry Barry, John Frederick, Steven Whittlesey, Otto Kirchner, Captain Peter Gronwall, Bruce Bigger, Lewis Langell, Ted McCutcheon, Creighton Holden, Paul Lydy, Maurice Jackson, Edward Middleton, Bernard Bast, John Anderson, Dr. Joseph Beer, Lillian Jackson Braun, Robert Carr, Felix Gabryel, David Herweyer, Donald Saari, Donald Pas, Hal Stein, Edward Posey, R.J. Rourke, Russel Breckenridge, Thomas Hensler, Jim Schudel, and Captain Sherwood Anderson.

Without the help of the following institutions from which much of the research data came, this book would not have been possible: The Dossin Great Lakes Museum, Detroit, Michigan; The Great Lakes Historical Society, Vermilion, Ohio; United States Coast Guard; The Manitowoc Maritime Museum, Manitowoc, Wisconsin; The Burton Historical Collection, Detroit Public Library, Detroit, Michigan; Museum of Arts and History, Port Huron, Michigan; Fort Malden Museum, Amherstburg, Ontario; Erie County Historical Society, Erie, Pennsylvania; Metropolitan Public Library, Toronto, Ontario; Public Archives, National Library, Ottawa, Ontario; Toledo Public Library; Sombra Township Museum, Sombra, Ontario; Macomb County Historical Society, Mt. Clemens, Michigan; American Shipbuilding Co.; Historical Society of Michigan, Ann Arbor, Michigan; United States Steel Co.; Pilot House Museum, Corruna, Ontario.

Preface

Long before my career as a marine artist began, I realized the lack of readily available information on many of the historic and nostalgic ships of the Great Lakes, both in the pictorial form and in literature. At that time, not having access to the information contained in marine museums, I discovered how difficult it was for the average person, not acquainted with any historical institution, to acquire this knowledge. A true gap existed between the accessible museum data and the material at the fingertips of the interested party. About the same time, my personal interest in Great Lakes lore exploded. Diving headlong into this fascinating research, I found that many others also were yearning for a glimpse at the maritime past that was seemingly lost or buried.

Not attempting to necessarily fill this gap, I began work on a few selected Great Lakes vessels through the help of the late Robert E. Lee, former curator of the Dossin Great Lakes Museum in Detroit. When merely ankle deep into the first project (Tashmoo), the idea of an entire series came to mind, and the work on these subjects began under the name of Great Lakes History in Art. Lithograph prints were made from the original paintings and sold through various dealers and galleries.

During the research for each painting, I collected documents, photographs, and other artifacts from each ship. Together with these treasures and so many very interesting facts about each vessel, I felt that after my painting project was completed, it would be a shame not to share this information with others. Thus, the book was in the making long ago. Here then is contained a digest of information on the selected subjects in the Great Lakes series now a part of Maritime History in Art.

J. Clary

Contents

TASHMOO

For you bouquets and ribboned wreaths,
For you the shores a-crowding.

Walt Whitman
"O Captain! My Captain!"

The first decade of the 1900s was notable for producing today's nostalgic memories of the Gibson girl and vaudeville. More important, that period was marked by the decline of the horse and buggy, the growth of the automobile industry, and the beginnings of aerial flight. In terms of recreation, people in that decade eagerly awaited the "good old summertime" with all its unique playtime opportunities. Riding bicycles, going on picnics, and watching baseball games were highly popular pastimes which occupied many persons through many leisure hours. Throughout the Great Lakes region, it was only natural that residents would take advantage of the fun that could be found on the big lakes. Wealthier individuals owned summer homes on Lake St. Clair, or on the St. Clair Flats, an area known to many as the "Paradise of the Great Lakes." Those not so financially solvent spent their vacations in any of the numerous resort hotels in the area. But those unable to afford either the expense of a summer home or a hotel vacation luxuriated in a trip aboard one of the many excursion boats that plied the Great Lakes and the Detroit and St. Clair Rivers.

Excursion boating enjoyed much success as a form of recreation in the early 1900s because it was readily available and modestly priced. Various steamship lines offered a variety of schedules and activities that appealed to a wide range of people. The White Star Lines and D & C Lines had numerous ships that offered many and varied summertime trips. The passengers of 1908, for instance, could use these boats as floating resort hotels or as transportation from one point to another or as week long trips with many stops where new towns could be explored. As their whims might dictate, they could select a seven day cruise, a weekend jaunt, or a day's outing. They could steam to Buffalo, sail to Port Huron or cruise to Mackinac. They could stop and stay at any port along the way, then be picked up by the same ship, or some other for the return. What a glorious era!

They could bask in the noonday sun and a bit later, after a nap, frolic under the stars. On board, they could dine in the most elegant "New York" style restaurants with fine table linens and real silverware and real live roses or carnations on the table. They could picnic on their own homemade wine and bread and cheeses and fruits brought in their own picnic baskets. During the day they could contentedly, lazily, watch the passing shoreline and evenings dance merrily to the music of a live dance band. Steamboating it was, and given a week of it no human, then or now, could avoid relaxation, joyful play and a good night's sleep when done.

Foremost among the steamers of that generation was the well-known and much loved *Tashmoo*. Owned by the White Star Line, she was fondly known to many as "The Glass Hack," "The Tash," and "The Queen of the St. Clair River." Frank Kirby, the noted marine architect, was commissioned to draw up the *Tashmoo's* blueprints in 1898. The *Tashmoo* was supposed to be a ship that would transport great numbers of persons from Detroit to the northern resort areas. Her trim hull was launched at Wyandotte, Michigan in December, 1899, and during that winter the ship was fitted with the finest appointments to provide a luxury previously unknown to passengers of sidewheel steamers. The *Tashmoo*, in fact, was one of the early members of that elegant tribe of happy steamboats that had reached beyond simple transportation and had arrived at luxury. Her stately decks were abundantly appointed with polished mahogany furniture and fine carpeting. Two grand pianos graced the main salon. Throughout, no expense was spared. By the spring of 1900, she was fully equipped and ready for trial runs, first on Lake St. Clair and then on Lake Erie. By June 11, 1900, she was ready for service and that day officially began a 36-year illustrious, carefree, often exciting career during which she would carry many very important people and participate in many noteworthy events.

During those early years, to say that the *Tashmoo's* schedule was a busy one was a gross understatement. In 1908, for example, "The Glass Hack," the name settled on this fine ship because it had more than 600 windows which afforded passengers of this "water taxi" a constant shoreline view, made a complete round trip daily from Detroit to Port Huron. Leaving Detroit at 8:30 a.m., the ship would arrive in Port Huron five-and-a-half hours and twenty stops later. Her longest stop, in St. Clair, was only thirty minutes while her briefest pause at Gus Trautz's Hotel near Harsen's Island was an incredible three minutes. When upbound at the shorter stops, her big paddle wheels would continue to churn the water while she loaded scrambling, excited passengers. By 3:45 p.m., the *Tashmoo* would be slipping south from Port Huron, following her morning schedule in reverse and arriving back at her Griswold Street berth in Detroit by 8:30 p.m. on time! She maintained this almost unbelievable pace day after day, weekends included, during the summer months from the middle of June through September. Think of the maintenance efforts, the food replenishment, the fuel banking, the bookwork that made

TASHMOO

STEAM WHISTLE
FROM THE PASSENGE
STEAMSHIP "TASHMO
YEAr BUILT.1900 FOR
THE WHITE STAR LINE
DETROIT, MICHIGAN.

The *Tashmoo's* whistle above, is made of brass. It is nearly four-and-a-half feet long and weighs 150 pounds. Right, the whistle is being blown in this photo of the pilot house. Photo courtesy Dr. Robert Clifford.

The Meaning Of Tashmoo

In researching the history of the *Tashmoo,* I discovered many interesting theories on the origin of this unusual name. The most common story told of a legendary Indian prince of this name who possessed great strength and courage. Many other ideas involved tales of a super-athlete. But I was unable to find any verification on the origin of the name, other than the fact that it was a reference to "Tashmoo Park."

On the advice of William J. Kubiac, an expert on the Indians of the Great Lakes, I went to Walpole Island in an attempt to track down the legend, although, according to Kubiac, there was a good chance that Tashmoo was not even part of the Ojibway language. At the Council Office I was directed to several of the elder inhabitants, but no one had ever heard the word "Tashmoo."

I left, thinking the theory about the Indian prince at least *sounded* plausible. But on the way to the bridge I spotted a small building with the sign, "Indian Language Center" on it. Elated at the possibilities this offered, I rushed into the office only to find that they had already been called by the ladies at the Council Office and could be of no help. I asked if they had an Ojibway dictionary, and the lady handed me the book: "A Manual for Missionaries & Others Employed among the Ojibway Indians." Using every word we could think of, we tried to match any sensible combination for a definition. Strong, Apollo, big, athelete. Nothing fit. I then asked the lady to find a word in Ojibway that would sound like Tashmoo. To my amazement, I was told that the first one or two letters of every Ojibway word is not pronounced. After reading aloud many words from different parts of the book the lady said the word "Aunwashemo" (pronounced New Weshemo) which means to rest! "That's it," I shouted. Pronounced quickly, "New Weshemo" sounds exactly like Tashmoo, and I had read that the Indians on Walpole Island welcomed Indians from other nations to stop and rest during their journey between lakes, and also that Tashmoo Park was billed in old advertisements as a "resting place." Thus, I realized I had rediscovered the true meaning of the word Tashmoo.

Above, the *Tashmoo* is under tow following an incident when she once ran aground near Algonac, Michigan. Photo courtesy Detroit Free Press. Right, such extras were sold at the bath house at Tashmoo Park. The Indian knife, opposite, also was sold there.

WHITE STAR ★ NAVIGATION CO

BATHING EXTRAS

GOOD THIS DATE ONLY

5¢	EXTRA TOWEL
10¢	BATHING CAP
10¢	STOCKINGS

CASHIER'S STUB

Form PK. 40

No. 963

sweet, beadwork, and moccasins to the tourists.

Although the *Tashmoo's* voyages followed a routine that met the needs of local folks, occasionally her schedule was totally revised to meet the needs of more eminent passengers. On two particular occasions, the *Tashmoo's* schedule was amended because of such guests. On June 9, 1900, two days prior to the opening of her official public service, the ship hosted Admiral George "Damn the Torpedos" Dewey. The valourous admiral had just returned from his successful conquest of the Philippines during the Spanish-American war, and was a national hero. In a spirit of great celebration, The *Tashmoo*, flying the Admiral's four-star flag above her pilot house, sailed from Cleveland for what would be her home port in Detroit. She carried the elite of Detroit's society as well as the Admiral and his escorts. As a 17-gun salute from the Navy gunboat, *U.S.S. Michigan*, resounded through the air, the *Tashmoo* departed from the dock accompanied by an array of ships and yachts including the revenue cutter *Fessenden*. The *Tashmoo* entered the Detroit River, proceeded upstream past Belle Isle, past Windmill Point, through Lake St. Clair, and into the St. Clair Flats, then turned back on the same course and headed back to her berth in Detroit.

This fanfare of arrival was topped two years later when her decks quaked with the roar of a 21-gun salute for President Theodore Roosevelt. On September 2, 1902, Roosevelt, the 26th President of the United States, came to Detroit to speak to Spanish-American War veterans. Because of her splendor, the *Tashmoo* was selected to take the President and his party on a sight-seeing tour of the city's skyline. With the President's blue and gold flag flying from her mainmast, the *Tashmoo* carried the illustrious group of dignitaries up and down the river till evening.

In her lifetime, just as the *Tashmoo* was involved with prominent people, she likewise became the central figure in other momentous events. Two of these were tests of her speed and strength. Whereas the first was a contest in which the *Tashmoo's* speed would be measured against a rival steamer, the second was a struggle in which the ship's strength would be pitted against the violent forces of nature. As fate would dictate, she would be victorious in only one of these endeavors. First, the race:

In the early 1900s one of the most thrilling and famous races on the Great Lakes occurred between the *Tashmoo* and the *City of Erie*. Most certainly it was an interesting encounter since both boats boasted excellence in speed. In fact, the *City of Erie*, just two years older than the *Tashmoo*, acquired the reputation of being the fastest ship on the Great Lakes. Nicknamed the "Honeymoon Special," she had attained some record speeds while carrying newlyweds east from Detroit and Cleveland on regular voyages to Niagara Falls. But speed also was an attribute of the *Tashmoo*, and she was frequently called "The White Flyer." Naturally, a race had to take place.

The stage had been set in September, 1900, when a friendly race between the *City of Chicago* and the *City of Milwaukee* took place on

Above, the pavilion at Tashmoo Park.
Right, one of the steering wheels that
belonged to this grand steamer.

Lake Michigan. The *City of Chicago* had been triumphant and was hailed by her supporters as the fastest ship on Great Lakes waters. To refute this claim, one Detroit newspaper maintained that at least nine ships could surpass the *City of Chicago*, and listed the nine in the article, however, the list for some reason failed to include the *Tashmoo*. The president of the White Star Lines, Aaron A. Parker, was furious at the oversight and in a public statement the next day offered $1000 to any ship that could beat his White Flyer. In fact, he said, the *Tashmoo* was the swiftest boat on fresh waters. That was too much for Thomas F. Newman, general manager of the Cleveland and Buffalo Transit Company, who readily accepted the challenge on behalf of the *City of Erie* and quickly matched the wager. The winner would earn the right to donate the money to the charity of his choice in his home city.

That winter it was decided that the race itself would cover a predetermined course covering 94 statute miles from Cleveland to Erie, Pennsylvania along the south shore of Lake Erie. Public excitement grew because both boats were fairly evenly matched. The *City of Erie*, for example, weighed 2500 gross tons, had a length of 316 feet and a beam of 44 feet. The *Tashmoo* was smaller, but very trim. With a weight of 1344 gross tons, the ship was 308 feet in length and had a beam of 37 feet. Still, the *Erie* held a territorial advantage, for she was racing on home grounds and was totally familiar with the course. The *Erie* also held a tactical advantage because her crew usually steered by compass, a skill seldom used by the pilot of the *Tashmoo*, who was accustomed to steering daytime courses by sight. Both of these factors would be significant in the outcome of the race.

On the morning of the big event an air of excitement was evident in Cleveland as throngs lined the city's docks and enthusiastic boaters in the harbor awaited the race. The two ships headed for the starting line and when a cannon signalled the start of the race, the *City of Erie*, immediately took the lead. But the *Tashmoo* came up fast and in the open waters of the lake, forged ahead to take a three length lead. But being five miles from shore and in a shallow lake, the *Tashmoo's* handicap soon became evident. Her helmsman's inability to steer by compass and his unfamiliarity with the water depth caused him to falter. This might have been overcome, but a greater misfortune now befell "The White Flyer." One of her condensers began to overheat and she was forced to reduce speed while her crew worked to correct the problem. The *City of Erie*, puffing along behind, was quick to capitalize on the *Tashmoo's* problems and soon took command of the race by twelve lengths. With her condenser repaired, The *Tashmoo* again steamed up to full speed and began to gain on her opponent. With the *Erie* in the lead, the *Tashmoo* now accelerated to even greater speed than before, and to the obvious relief of her supporters she began to rapidly close the gap. Closer and closer she came and the expectant crowd watched anxiously for a photo finish. But the big lead the *City of Erie* had developed proved just too much and she crossed the finish line 45 seconds ahead of the *Tashmoo*. Although she had lost the race, she had shown herself to be faster at full speed

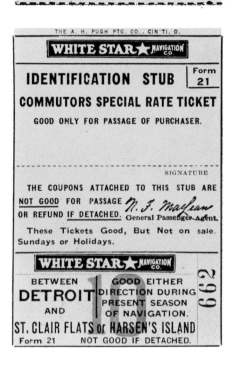

Above, a merchant's raffle ticket for a free drawing that was held at a Lincoln Park Day celebration, an excursion ticket from the White Star Navigation Company, and an admission ticket to Tashmoo Park.

Above left, a winter storm in 1927 carried the *Tashmoo* up the Detroit River. But she was finally stopped by the Belle Isle Bridge. Photo by the Detroit *News*. Left, a cup and saucer from the *Tashmoo*. Above, a sketch of the famous race between the *Tashmoo* and the *City of Erie* that was held on Lake Erie in 1901.

and on this basis, her owners offered $10,000 for a rematch. But the *City of Erie's* owners sensed they'd be better off not to try again and rejected all future confrontations at any stakes.

Though thwarted in her bid to outrun the *City of Erie*, the "White Flyer" ultimately triumphed in a memorable, and somewhat humorous battle with nature. On December 8, 1927, Detroit was buffeted by gale force winds and frigid temperatures during one of the worst blizzards in the city's history. Casualties were numerous as the local papers testified in their accounts of missings ships and lost men. According to reports by the Detroit *Free Press*, the 60 mile per hour winds were so overpowering that they literally blew waters from the Detroit River upstream into Lake St. Clair, causing the river's water level to drop a full four feet! The strain proved too great for the dock at Griswold Street where the *Tashmoo* was moored for the winter and all her lines snapped. Trailing a string of pilings like a strange necklace, "The Queen" bobbed upstream. Seeking a companion she crashed into the ferry *Promise*, and caused this boat to break from her moorings as well. Together, they continued toward Lake St. Clair, and it was only because she took a wrong turn and got jammed against the concrete abutment of the Belle Isle Bridge, that frantic workmen were able to get a line on the runaway. But freedom tasted too heady, and she wasn't finshed yet. Two tug boats were able to attach lines to the vessel and turn her head homeward, but after a short run, she broke loose from the tugs and once again headed for the bridge. Luckily another collision was averted as the tugs sped to her rescue. Although damaged, "The Queen" survived her seven-hour ordeal, gave up her necklace of pilings, got a new face and some paint and by June of the following year she was back on her regular schedule. The *Tashmoo's* experience, however, foreshadowed her end eight-and-a-half years later. On June 18, 1936, the ship started down the Detroit River on a moonlight charter. All went well at first, and the cruise continued all the way to Sugar Island, where her passengers disembarked for a brief stay. Then as the ship was turning around to head back upstream she struck a huge boulder in the Sugar Island channel and began to take on volumes of water. Oblivious to the ship's plight her passengers were told merely that the *Tashmoo* was having some engine trouble. Struggling against the ship's wound, the captain was able to dock at Amherstburg, Ontario, where her passengers casually disembarked. But it wasn't long after the last one got ashore that the ship settled to the bottom in 14 feet of water. Although dealt a serious blow, the underwater damage was slight and salvage attempts began a short time later. Unfortunately, in their hurry, the salvage crew raised one end too quickly and her keel was broken, thus ending the career of this most special vessel. The Flats would never again see the *Tashmoo's* colorful flags and windowed sides, but even today, some of her loyal supporters along the old route insist that on warm moonlit summer nights they can still see the ship's reflections dancing on the water and also hear the strains of soft music from her orchestra filtering through the still air. □

Above, a baggage claim check from Tashmoo Park.

26

LABOR DAY AT RIVER CRAB · ST. CLAIR, MICHIGAN

CHUCK MUER'S

JIM CLARY'S

GRAND OLE TASHMOO WHISTLE BLOW

held this year in honor of

ROBERT E. LEE

who has recently completed a distinguished career as
CURATOR OF THE DOSSIN GREAT LAKES MUSEUM

Hear actual whistles from famous excursion steamers
TASHMOO ● CITY OF BUFFALO ● CHRISTOPHER COLUMBUS
Freighters RENOWN and VERONA
Train Whistles ● Factory Whistles ● Many More

BLOW THEM YOURSELF
Bring your own and enter for ribbons

MONDAY ● LABOR DAY ● NOON to 4 P.M. ● Awards at 2 P.M.
Chuck Muer's RIVER CRAB on the St. Clair River north of St. Clair, Mich.
BEER — BARBECUE

Left, the Grand Ole Tashmoo Whistle Blow is held annually on Labor Day at the River Crab restaurant in St. Clair, Michigan. Below, the tragic scene of the *Tashmoo* when she sank in 14 feet of water at Amhertsburg, Ontario in 1936. Photo by William James Taylor.

CITY OF DETROIT III

These summer clouds she sets for sail
The sun is her masthead light,
She tows the moon like a pinnace frail
Where her phosphor wake churns bright.

William Vaughn Moody
"Glouchester Moors"

Historically, the second decade of the 20th Century was not a peaceful one. In Europe, the "war to end all wars" was being fought, and here in the United States, as the country teetered on the brink of involvement during the middle years of the decade, the debate over peace or war was finally resolved on April 6, 1917 when Congress voted for war. But domestically, the decade also was marked by great political and social unrest. It was a period marked by "reform." The Progressive Movement, women's suffrage, and the awakening of the nation's social conscience, were but a few of the struggles which faced the American people.

Recreationally, however, the country still sought the "good life" in spite of world tensions, and the tranquility which dominated the entertainment scene of the preceding years continued on into the new decade, as well, as over the course of these years the public was lulled by the music of Irving Berlin, entertained by the lavish productions of the Ziegfield Follies, and amused by the antics of Charlie Chaplin, the Keystone Cops, and the other great comedians of the silent movies.

On the Great Lakes, excursion boating remained a very popular and pleasurable diversion. Steamship lines were highly competitive and were constantly battling each other to become known as the "most popular" or the "most successful." To achieve such lofty status, it was not uncommon for the various lines to add new ships to their fleet, and thereby establish new records in size, speed, or elegance simply with the addition of the new ship. Consequently, while the *Tashmoo* had set the record as being the longest passenger ship on the Detroit waterfront in 1901, and the *Put-In-Bay* had claimed the record as being the largest excursion boat in the Detroit area in 1911, the *City of Detroit III,* when launched in 1912, had become the largest sidewheeler in the world. From stem to stern she measured 470 feet or the approximate length of two Detroit city blocks.

Breaking a record, however, was not the only similarity the *City of Detroit III* shared with her notable rivals. Although all three steamships were owned by different companies, all were designed by the same marine architect, Frank E. Kirby. And like the beloved *Tashmoo* in her day, the *City of Detroit III* also possessed an interior architectural style and decor of unsurpassed elegance. She was truly a beautiful ship. But here the similarity ends, for although both excursion boats occasionally crossed paths in their journeys up and down the inland waterway system and the big lakes themselves, they usually traveled different routes. While the *Tashmoo* would usually set a northward course from Detroit into Lake St. Clair, the *City of Detroit III* sailed south to Lake Erie and then east, making the trip from Detroit to Buffalo. In terms of distance traveled, the *Tashmoo* followed a shorter route, so that she could easily make a round trip in twelve hours, a splendid day-long excursion. On the other hand, a cruise aboard the *City of Detroit III* would frequently last overnight or even longer if she were chartered. Finally, although the career of the *City of Detroit III* would exceed that of the *Tashmoo* by eight years, her 44-year history was somewhat less eventful. Nevertheless, her passengers held her in high esteem.

The *City of Detroit III* was owned by the Detroit and Cleveland Navigation Company, a well-established line which took great pride in its grand tradition, as well as in its good reputation. Throughout the long history of the company, its fleet had consistently provided first class service for its passengers. The D & C Line also was known for its ability to achieve superlatives: its ships were frequently the largest; its traffic was generally the heaviest; and its length of service was nearly the longest. When the D & C Steamboat Line began operations in 1850, the only route taken by its two wooden steamships was between the cities of Detroit and Cleveland, and thus it is from these first two port cities that the company got its name. At that time, however, rather than offering luxury excursion cruises, the company was providing westward passage for the migrating settlers. But in the decades to come, the amount of ships, the number of routes, and the length of those routes would greatly increase, so that eventually, the D & C liners would carry thousands of passengers eastward to Buffalo, northward to Mackinac, and westward to Chicago on the finest pleasure trips of the day. And throughout those long years, the D & C Line prospered where others had failed. But ultimately, the company's demise took place along with the decline of excursion boating. In the latter half of the 1940s, D & C's business, like that of the other lines, had become an unprofitable venture. If the company had merely suffered the negative economic effects that World War II had inflicted on the industry, it might have been able to succeed. However, a disastrous accident combined with this factor to force the dissolution of the company.

In June, 1950, the D & C's *City of Cleveland III*, the sister ship of the *City of Detroit III*, collided with an ocean-going freighter in Lake Huron. Following the accident the D & C liner was declared a major

Above, a baggage tag from the D & C steamer *City of Detroit III.*

CITY OF DETROIT III

disaster by the Coast Guard. Thus she would have to be totally rebuilt. But this was simply too expensive a proposition for an already financially troubled company. Worse still, the D & C Line was found to be responsible for the accident and therefore the beleaguered company was plagued with several major lawsuits. Unable to survive such adversity, the company ceased operations at the close of the 1950 season, after providing 100 years of valiant service on the Great Lakes. The D & C Line was then formally disbanded in 1960. Although the company's last years were not so illustrious, the name D & C would continue to evoke fond memories of gaiety and grace whenever it was mentioned.

In addition to sharing the good reputation of her parent company, the *City of Detroit III* also acquired a special social status from the fame of her esteemed ancestors. The first *City of Detroit* was constructed in 1878, and at that time, she was the finest excursion liner on the route, as well as the largest. Her career would endure more than 30 years, but for only 15 of those years would she sail under the name of *City of Detroit*. For the latter half of her service, she would be known as the *City of the Straits*. This change occurred in 1893, in order to avoid confusion with another *City of Detroit*, which had been built in 1889. This second *City of Detroit* continued to follow the tradition of excellence established by the D & C Line by setting a record for length which she maintained for some time. Even as late as 1910, she was still the second largest ship in her company's fleet, excelling in speed and boasting handsome accommodations.

When the *D-III*, as she was affectionately called, was introduced in

Above, the ship's main dining room, and a D & C menu. Designed in the shape of a fish, the menu is shown first closed and then opened.

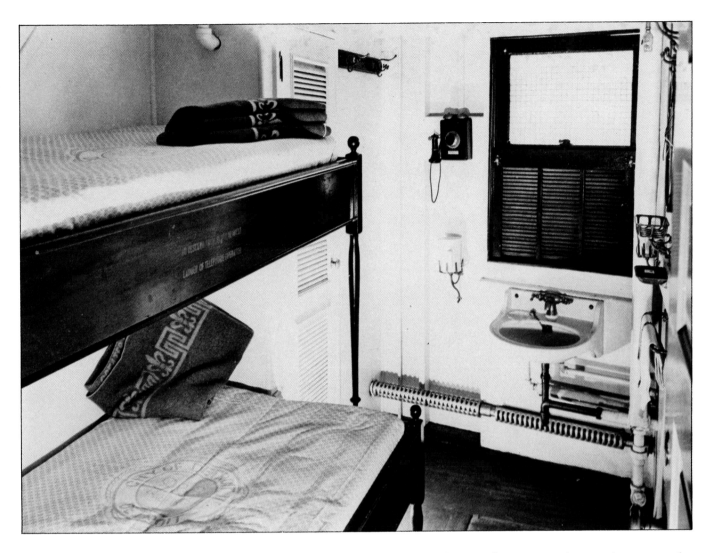

The accommodations above were for passengers who traveled second class. Left, a water pitcher, a pair of corn holders, a coffee urn, and other items of tableware from the D & C Line.

1912, not only was she the largest sidewheeler in the world, but she was also the grandest liner on the lakes. Her accomplishments would be short-lived, however, because the following year, the rival Cleveland and Buffalo Transit Company launched their majestic 500-foot long *Seeandbee*, a beautiful ship containing four decks which would overshadow her glory and popularity. Nonetheless, the *City of Detroit III* was indeed a grand lady.

Her black hull was a vivid, yet tasteful contrast to her light cream colored cabins, while the presence of the large D & C gold insignia and her gold-lettered name contributed to the over-all dignity of her stately outward appearance. Her interior atmosphere, from the elaborate, classical architecture to the ornate decor, also abounded in richness. Some of her public sitting rooms for example, had high, beautifully painted ceilings which were supported by massive, ornate pillars. Some of these pillars were adorned with intricately carved heads of various mythological figures. And throughout the ship, fine wood beamed ceilings and paneled walls added yet another touch of elegance to this regal setting.

Her three decks contained sections of spacious public rooms as well as large-sized private staterooms. Of the public rooms, perhaps one of the most interesting and the most popular among the

On the D & C dinner menu above, the letters from the company logo also stood for "Delicious Cuisine," another trademark of the line.

passengers was located on the top deck. This room, known as the Gothic Room, provided the passengers with both a lounge and a smoking area. One of its unique features was a beautiful Tiffany stained glass window which portrayed the French explorer Robert Cavelier de la Salle as he was leading his small party of explorers in the Michigan wilderness under the watchful eyes of the Indians. Also, partially encircled by glass windows, the perimeter of the room contained several observation booths that permitted passengers to enjoy the passing scenery. A pipe organ in the room provided another form of rousing entertainment, and a fireplace made the

room nice and cozy on cool evenings.

The private staterooms, too, were outstanding examples of the company's attempt to provide all of the modern conveniences for its passengers. While only 25 rooms contained full baths and private verandas, and 50 staterooms were equipped with private toilets, all 600 staterooms contained hot and cold running water. And each room had a telephone, although it could be used only while the ship was docked. Electricity was another modern convenience, and at night, the ship was ablaze with hundreds of electric lamps. Four hundred such lamps lighted the dining room alone.

This photo of the *City of Detroit III* was taken as she moved through the locks at Sault Ste. Marie, Michigan. Photo courtesy William Hayward collection.

DETROIT & CLEVELAND NAVIGATION CO.

A Vacation in the Great Lakes Country

OFFICERS
A. A. Schantz, President
J. T. McMillan, Executive Vice-President and Treasurer
C. L. Perkins, General Manager
E. H. McCracken, General Passenger Agent

STEAMER SCHEDULES
Improved Service and Increased Capacity
Large Steamers on All Divisions
Steamers Operate on Eastern Standard Time

DETROIT and BUFFALO DIVISION
Overnight Service
STR. GREATER DETROIT, "Leviathan of the Great Lakes"
STR. GREATER BUFFALO, "Majestic of the Great Lakes"

May 1st to November 1st

Lv. DETROIT daily - - - - - - - -	5:00 P. M.
Ar. BUFFALO daily - - - - - - -	8:00 A. M.
Lv. BUFFALO daily - - - - - - -	6:00 P. M.
Ar. DETROIT daily - - - - - - - -	9:00 A. M.

DETROIT and CLEVELAND DIVISION
Overnight Service
April 1st to December 1st
STR. CITY OF DETROIT III
STR. CITY OF CLEVELAND III } Giants of the Great Lakes

Lv. DETROIT daily - - - - - -	11:30 P. M.
Ar. CLEVELAND daily - - - - - -	6:45 A. M.
Lv. CLEVELAND daily - - - - - -	11:30 P. M.
Ar. DETROIT daily - - - - - - -	6:45 A. M.

Daylight service daily (except Sundays, July 4 and Labor Day, September 2,) From June 25 to September 3

Lv. DETROIT - - - - - - - -	11:00 A. M.
Ar. CLEVELAND - - - - - - -	5:45 P. M.
Lv. CLEVELAND - - - - - - -	11:00 A. M.
Ar. DETROIT - - - - - - - -	5:45 P. M.

DETROIT and CHICAGO
(via Mackinac Island and St. Ignace)
Overnight Service
Leaving Detroit June 25th to September 5th
Leaving Chicago June 27th to September 7th

	STR. EASTERN STATES	STR. WESTERN STATES	
Lv. DETROIT	Tues. Thur. Sat.	....	1:30 p. m., E. T.
Ar. Mackinac Island	Wed. Fri.	Sun.	9:15 a. m., "
Lv. Mackinac Island	Wed. Fri.	Sun.	9:45 a. m., "
Ar. St. Ignace	Wed. Fri.	Sun.	10:15 a. m., "
Lv. St. Ignace	Wed. Fri.	Sun.	11:30 a. m., "
Ar. Mackinac Island	Wed. Fri.	Sun.	12:00 noon "
Lv. Mackinac Island	Wed. Fri.	Sun.	12:30 p. m., "
Ar. CHICAGO	Thur. Sat.	Mon.	9:00 a. m., "
Lv. CHICAGO	Mon. Thur.	Sat.	2:30 p. m., "
Ar. Mackinac Island	Tues. Fri.	Sun.	10:30 a. m., "
Lv. Mackinac Island	Tues. Fri.	Sun.	11:15 a. m., "
Ar. St. Ignace	Tues. Fri.	Sun.	11:45 a. m., "
Lv. St. Ignace	Tues. Fri.	Sun.	12:30 p. m., "
Ar. Mackinac Island	Tues. Fri.	Sun.	1:00 p. m., "
Lv. Mackinac Island	Tues. Fri.	Sun.	1:30 p. m., "
Ar. Detroit	Wed. Sat.	Mon.	8:00 a. m., "

LOCAL FARES
Meals and Berth Extra

Detroit, Mich.

	Buffalo	Cleve.	Cleveland Day Rate
One Way	$ 5.00	$ 3.00	$ 2.50
Round Trip	10.00	5.50	......
Excess Baggage, per 100 lbs.	.85	.50	.50

Meals and Berth Included

Mack. Is., Mich.

	Buffalo	Cleve.	Detroit	St. Ignace	Chicago
One Way	$25.50	$22.00	$16.00	$ 0.60	$16.00
Round Trip	49.00	41.50	30.00	......	30.00
Excess Baggage, per 100 lbs.	2.50	2.15	1.65	.25	1.65

Meals and Berth Included

St. Ignace, Mich.

	Buffalo	Cleve.	Detroit	Mack. Is.	Chicago
One Way	$25.50	$22.00	$16.00	$ 0.60	$16.00
Round Trip	49.00	41.50	30.00	......	30.00
Excess Baggage, per 100 lbs.	2.50	2.15	1.65	.25	1.65

Meals and Berth Included

Chicago, Ill.

	Buffalo	Cleve.	Detroit	Mack. Is.	St. Ignace
One Way	$40.50	$37.00	$31.00	$16.00	$16.00
Round Trip	79.00	.71.50	60.00	30.00	30.00
Excess Baggage, per 100 lbs.	4.15	3.80	3.30	1.65	1.65

Fares do not include luncheon on steamer at Detroit or Chicago.

Meals and Berth Charges
(Either Direction)
Between Buffalo, N. Y., and Detroit, Mich. (Buffalo Division)
Sleeping accommodations

Corridor Rooms, $3.50. Lower berth in Corridor Room, $2.00. Upper berth in Corridor Room, $1.50. Single berth Corridor Room, $3.00. Deck Rooms, $4.00. Lower berth in Deck Room, $2.25. Upper berth in Deck Room, $1.75. Deck Rooms with two berths and toilet, $5.00. Deck Rooms with two berths, shower bath and toilet, $6.00. Parlors $9.50, $11.00, $12.50, $15.00. Berths sold only in $3.50 and $4.00 rooms.

MEALS: Breakfast—Hours 6:30 A. M. to 9:00 A. M.—Club and a la Carte. Dinner—Hours 5:00 P. M. to 12:00 P. M.—a la Carte, also Table d'Hote, from 5:00 P. M. to 8:00 P. M. Price $1.50. In addition to the above service, a "Coffee Shop" is also available during Breakfast and Dinner Hours.

Between Cleveland, Ohio, and Detroit, Mich. (Cleveland Div.)
Sleeping accommodations

Corridor Rooms, $3.50. Lower berth in Corridor Room, $2.00. Upper berth in Corridor Room, $1.50. Deck Rooms, $4.00. Lower berth in Deck Room, $2.25. Upper berth in Deck Room, $1.75. Extra large Deck Rooms, $4.50. Deck Rooms with toilet, $5.00. Parlors $7.00, $9.00, $10.00, $11.00, $14.00. Berths sold only in $3.50 and $4.00 rooms.

MEALS: Breakfast—Hours 6:00 A. M. to 8:30 A. M.—Club and a la Carte. Dining Room is also open from 8:30 P. M. to 12:30 A. M. for a la Carte service.

Between Detroit, Mich., Mackinac Island, Mich., St. Ignace, Mich., and Chicago, Ill. (Chicago Division)

MEAL HOURS: Breakfast—7:00 A. M. to 9:00 A. M. Luncheon—12:00 noon to 2:00 P. M. Dinner—6:00 P. M. to 8:00 P. M.

BERTHS: Fares include berth in ordinary stateroom.

ONE PASSENGER desiring the exclusive use of a stateroom or parlor on steamers plying in either direction between Detroit, Mackinac Island, St. Ignace, Michigan, and Chicago, Illinois, will require one and one-half passenger fare which includes meals and berth plus the cost of additional charge for room or parlor.

Children under twelve and over five years of age, half fare; under five, if accompanied by adult, free transportation.

Opposite, a Detroit and Cleveland Navigation Company schedule. Above, the more spacious first class staterooms even had their own private balcony. Left, two examples of the elaborate decorations found on the *City of Detroit III*. The carved head of Bacchus, the Greek god of wine, adorned the surroundings of the palm courtroom, and the frog is actually a portion of a wall lamp that was used on the D & C liners.

Dancing was always a favorite pastime aboard the D & C steamers. These young couples may have been on a graduation cruise, a popular excursion offered by the company.

The *D-III* was also equipped with the latest safety innovations. This was essential because the "unsinkable" *Titanic* had been lost at sea in the north Atlantic only two months before the *City of Detroit III* was going to be launched. Following this tragic incident, the public was less than enthusiastic about sailing and the D & C Line, as well as the other companies, had to mount extensive advertising campaigns to overcome the skeptical attitude of the public. Her promotional advertisements emphasized all of her safety features, which included fire alarms, fire walls, and sprinkler systems. Additionally, passengers were constantly being reassured that the captain was in constant contact with shore and with passing ships via the Marconi wireless. Moreover, she carried more life jackets and lifeboats than necessary. Fire drills were also an accepted part of her excursion routine and her crew was well disciplined to act quickly and responsibly in all emergency situations.

Fortunately, the *City of Detroit III* was never forced to depend on any of her emergency equipment while making her normal run

between Detroit and Buffalo, although she was involved in a small crisis on her very first trial run. But this incident apparently was the only one which ever blemished her otherwise spotless record. As she departed from the shipyard in Detroit on May 30, 1912, she struck the *Joseph C. Suit*, a small package cargo steamer. This accident postponed her maiden voyage until June 26, 1912, when she sailed for Buffalo. This first trip marked the beginning of a long and honorable career, the majority of which would be spent making the Buffalo run. In 1924, she was transferred to the Detroit and Cleveland route, but in the 1940s, she returned to her original schedule, maintaining service between Detroit and Buffalo until the D & C Line terminated its operations in 1950. In September, 1956, after a long and undignified wait at her berth in Detroit, the *City of Detroit III* was stripped and dismantled. Yet, the proud legacy of this grand steamer remains, for a portion of her beautiful Gothic Room has been reconstructed at the Dossin Great Lakes Museum on Belle Isle in Detroit. □

No trip aboard the elegant *City of Detroit III* was complete without the captain leading the passengers on a promenade all around the deck to the music of "Shufflin Off To Buffalo."

PUT~IN~BAY

August for the people and their favorite islands,
Daily the steamers sidle up to meet
The effusive welcome of the pier.

W. H. Auden
"August for the People"

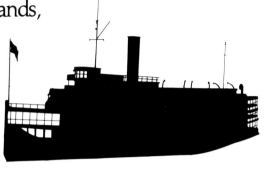

While excursion boating flourished on the Great Lakes in the decade between 1910 and 1920, another favorite form of recreation was sweeping the country, as people were rapidly being caught up in the dance craze. Dancing was a way of "letting go," and it was a contagious experience which captivated the attention and energies of young and old alike. In crowded ballrooms, dance halls, and gymnasiums, people enthusiastically performed the grizzly bear, the bunny hug and the turkey trot. Each dance step seemed to be more outrageous than the next and the only rule on the dance floor was "anything goes!" However, all of the jiggling and jouncing of these dances soon gave way to the swinging and swaying of the foxtrot, the tango and the castle walk. On the inland waterway system, connecting Lakes St. Clair and Erie, the Ashley and Dustin Lines company seized an opportunity to capitalize on this latest trend, as they commissioned a special excursion liner which would simultaneously supply its passengers with both the luxuries of cruising and the pleasures of dancing. The ship was the *Put-In-Bay,* and in her lifetime she would attain a popularity that would rival the success of the *Tashmoo.*

From the very beginning, there was no doubt that the *Put-In-Bay* was a dancing ship, since her most prominent feature was a ballroom which occupied the major portion of the promenade deck. Typical of the elegance and design of the entire ship, this room contained several innovative appointments that served to accommodate the continuous dancing activities of the passengers. The room even boasted a highly polished hardwood dance floor. While such flooring provided the ideal surface for dancers, some pessimistic observers predicted that the perpetual dampness of the lake would eventually cause the hardwood to buckle. Luckily, such gloomy predictions never materialized. And to make the dancers more comfortable, sliding glass doors were installed to fully enclose the room. These doors would remain open in pleasant weather so that the soft evening breezes could freely circulate through the room. Yet, in inclement weather they would be closed so that neither high winds nor rain would detract from the jovial atmosphere which prevailed inside.

The *Put-In-Bay* was also one of the finest excursion ships. In the observation area above the ballroom, many passengers would gather along the front and both sides of this room to have an excellent and unencumbered view of the water and the passing shoreline, while in the rear of this room several individual parlors offered privacy to those passengers seeking a more intimate rendezvous. Generally, however, an open and festive atmosphere pervaded all four decks of the *Put-In-Bay* so that the passengers could fully enjoy the sun, the moon and the stars, and the soft summer winds while on their cruise.

In addition to all of her fine appointments, the technical aspects of the *Put-In-Bay* were also indicative of the progress and innovation taking place in the shipbuilding industry. Whereas other steamers of her time were frequently sidewheelers, she was a propeller ship. The propeller made it possible for the ship to be easily maneuvered in close quarters, movements that might otherwise have been difficult for her 256-foot length and her 60 foot beam. She also possessed the latest advancements in safety, as the ship was equipped with a sprinkler system and fire alarm boxes were located throughout the ship in the event of a fire. And because she also had watertight bulkheads, her owners believed she was unsinkable. Fortunately, this lofty claim would never be challenged during her career.

Throughout her 38 years of service, the *Put-In-Bay* acquired a romantic reputation and endeared herself to her passengers. Part of this acclaim could be attributed to the fact that although she was primarily a day cruiser, she would frequently sail on moonlight cruises as well. Appropriately, then, on any given evening excursion, hundreds of participants and spectators in her ballroom would be charmed by the sounds of "On Moonlight Bay" which had become the ship's theme song. In fact, from the reminiscences of many of these same individuals who now fondly recall the numerous good times they shared on her decks, it is quite evident that her officers and approximately 100 crew members had succeeded in upholding their well known motto: "Rain or shine--always a good time on the big *S.S. Put-In-Bay.*" More specifically, some of the responsibility for cherished memories and for the *Put-In-Bay's* popularity as a dance boat belonged to George Finzer, one of the few bandleaders to ever play on the ship. Finzer not only led the musicians in pleasing and entertaining the passengers, he did it almost without interruption. Few people, if any, could match Finzer's record. There was nearly always non-stop music on every voyage, and moreover, he never missed one sailing in 38 years and was even present when the *Put-In-Bay* was set afire in 1953.

From her maiden voyage on June 17, 1911 until her service was terminated in 1949, the *Put-In-Bay* nearly always followed the same routine, except for a brief period when she took over making the

PUT-IN-BAY

Considered the pride of the Ashley and Dustin Steamship Company, here are three views of the beautiful *Put-In-Bay*, one of the most popular excursion liners of her day. Primarily a ship for dancing, her career lasted 38 years. The top two photos courtesy Dossin Great Lakes Museum Collection. The bottom photo courtesy Great Lakes Historical Society Collection.

Tashmoo's runs to Tashmoo Park on the St. Clair Flats, after that ship's demise in 1936. Her major duty was to shuttle up to as many as 3500 passengers on a single cruise of western Lake Erie, sailing from Detroit to Put-in-Bay on South Bass Island, then onward to Sandusky. This journey was essentially a trek through time as a portion of the route passed near two sites which were part of two separate conflicts in our history. The first and most important location is near Middle Sister Island which is located in the Canadian waters of Lake Erie between Detroit and Put-in-Bay. It was here in 1813 that Commodore Oliver Hazard Perry triumphantly led the United States to a victory over the British in the famous Battle of Lake Erie. After departing from Put-in-Bay, the steamer passed the second area of historic interest. Just before reaching Sandusky, Ohio, the *Put-In-Bay* advanced past a small group of islands in Sandusky Bay. Among them is Johnson's Island which served as a Union prison during the Civil War. Because the island prison provided ideal security, nearly 15,000 confederate soldiers were imprisoned there during the course of the war. And those prisoners who died during their confinement were buried in the cemetery which still remains today.

The favorite attraction of the passengers and by far the most popular point of the entire excursion, however, was the 1750-acre island community for which the ship was named: Put-in-Bay. Here a

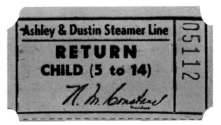

Left, the outside pages of a *Put-In-Bay* cruise brochure. "Just like an ocean cruise" was the claim made by her owners. It's doubtful that any of her passengers ever wanted their money back. Above, three tickets for the Ashley & Dustin Steamer Line.

small number of permanent residents lived in the quaint little town. At one time, the island also was the home of an actor's colony that had been established towards the westward shore. The colony has long since departed, but for a number of years, it contributed a great deal of interest and excitement to the over-all unique character of the island. In this attractive setting, the residents of the island were involved in such divergent business ventures as a vineyard and a fish hatchery. For the tourists, there was a dance hall and a roller rink, as well as other amusement spots, and the caves of the region were available for exploration by the more adventurous.

But it was the water which served as the island's greatest attraction, and there was a long toboggan slide at the swimming beach which contributed to the fun of the bathers. The area is also a perfect setting for boating, and an annual regatta has been held there for the past 88 years. It was with only 13 contenders and a total prize purse of $570, that the first international regatta ever held on the Great Lakes took place at Put-In-Bay on September 6, 1871. Today, the area is still the sight of the largest freshwater yachting activity of its kind, and each year the Interlake Yachting Association plays host to several hundred entrants in their annual regatta.

Put-in-Bay also has a national monument which serves as a testimonial to those who sacrificed their lives in the Battle of Lake

Erie. The Perry Memorial Monument, dedicated on September 10, 1913, to mark the centennial of Admiral Perry's courageous victory in that historic conflict, was opened to the public on June 13, 1915. The towering monolith stands 352 feet high, and the promenade on the top affords as many as 300 people a breathtaking view of the surrounding countryside. Since its opening the tall column also has served as a lifesaving beacon to those in peril on the lake.

While the ship was named for the island community, the origin of the name itself is quite interesting and a number of fascinating tales, some more believable than others, have evolved over the years to provide explanations. According to one imaginative theory, while sailing in the area, Commodore Perry once supposedly ordered his ship to "Put in the bay." Other sources dispute this explanation on the basis that the island was named long before Perry's arrival. More likely, the beginnings of the name can be traced to 1789 when South Bass Island was first charted. Although the area now known as Put-in-Bay wasn't listed on this map, the harbor was designated as Pudding Bay. According to one interpretation, this name evolved because the outline of the harbor resembled the shape of a pudding bag. And for the next few decades, the name appeared in a number of ways in various log books and letters. Finally, an old map of 1815, drawn up by reputable surveyors refers to the water surrounding South Bass Island as Put-in-Bay.

Whatever its origins, the familiar name of *Put-In-Bay* became synonymous with pleasure to millions of summertime vacationers. But inevitably, that pleasure, like so many other endeavors, must come to an end. Thus, long the favorite of sweethearts, the romantic ship *Put-In-Bay* finally ended her service in 1949, although steamboat service to the island resort continued into the early 1950s. Today, a ferry service takes visitors to the island. This beloved ship which had long provided so much enjoyment for so many then remained idle for the next few years. Ultimately, however, she was sold for scrap to satisfy tax claims pending against the company. Consequently, on October 3, 1953, with her flags at half mast, the ship was towed to Lake St. Clair, the familiar scene of so many a midnight rendezvous aboard her decks. It was almost as if a somber funeral ceremony was taking place because in a dignified manner, the salvage crew tried to set her afire. However, it seemed as though this grand lady was still trying to cling to those happier times for she refused to keep burning. In the end, such valiant efforts were finally overcome. As the evening wore on and the spectators who had lined the shore sadly turned for home, the *Put-In-Bay* finally caught fire. She met her inevitable demise in a blaze of glory as 150 foot flames leapt skyward. And although her steel hull and engines were sold for scrap, not all of this once proud and elegant liner was destroyed. Her bell was removed and placed at the Mariner's Church in Detroit. Thus deprived of life, the memory of the *Put-In-Bay* was destined to remain alive, nevertheless; as thousands will never forget those carefree, happy, and romantic cruises aboard her hospitable decks. □

ASHLEY & DUSTIN
STEAMER LINE

Special Ride

02631

O. J. Dustin
G. M.

MASTERS and WARDENS' COUNCIL
Districts One and Two

3rd MOONLIGHT RIDE

Enjoy an Evening of Masonic Fellowship

Beautiful Steamer Put-In-Bay

EMBARK at the FOOT of FIRST STREET

Monday, June 25, 1951 — 8:30 P. M.

Elger Harvey, Pres.   W. L. Johnson, Sec.

Adult Tickets $1.50   Orchestra Music

N⁰   664

Above, the only sad day in the glorious career of the *Put-In-Bay* occurred on October 3, 1953 when she was set afire in Lake St. Clair. Photo courtesy Dossin Great Lakes Museum Collection. Left, a special ride ticket, perhaps for a free trip, and a ticket for a chartered cruise.

SOUTH AMERICAN

"To chat, to walk a bit, to see an unexpected friend, to read, to drowse and dream, swung between the strenuous world you've left and the strenuous world that waits for you......where is life ever so lazy, as agreeable?"

A 1920s French Line Brochure

Someone once said that a trip aboard a big excursion vessel was like living in another world. All of your real-life cares and woes are left at the dock, waiting for your return, so that for the duration of the cruise, you and the people you meet aboard this floating Shangrila are transformed, for a few days at least, into a fun-loving, charitable, happy-go-lucky family of travelers. And someone else long ago affirmed the idea that a ship is truly a genuine person, a lady if you will, complete with her own mind, spirit, and character. If you share these views, and if you're somewhere in that time of life some people call middle age, you may fondly remember the *S.S. South American*. For she definitely was a lady, and she definitely stood for happiness, becoming the sweetheart at everyone's first glance, and then forever endearing herself to all those who briefly "escaped" the real world on one of her cruises.

Robert C. Davis was a general passenger agent for the Goodrich Transit Company in Chicago when he thought of the idea of long distance luxury cruises on the Great Lakes. And so, resigning from the company in 1912, Davis began promoting his idea heavily throughout the United States and Canada. An effective salesman, he quickly raised enough money, and in August of that year he formed the Chicago, Duluth, & Georgian Bay Transit Company with Charles Bour, William Black, and F.S. Smith. Davis was the president.

In the spring of 1913, the new company's first ship, the *North American* was launched at the Great Lakes Engineering Works, at Ecorse, Michigan. She was immediately hailed as a "model of modern shipbuilding." Public response was overwhelming and the need for another ship was obvious, so plans were immediately drawn up.

On February 1, 1914, hull number 133, the *South American* also was launched at the Ecorse yard and, once more it was quite apparent that her owners knew exactly what to offer the anxious excursion customer, for the ship was quickly accepted as the "sweetheart of the

Above, both sides of a good luck charm from the *South American,* the "sweetheart of the Lakes."

Lakes." Her maiden voyage began June 13, 1914, on a Detroit to Chicago run and a large crowd of Detroit residents turned out to see their beautiful lady off.

With an overall length of 321 feet, a beam of 47 feet, 10 inches, and a depth of 18 feet, 3 inches, this exclusive passenger boat had accommodations for 540 passengers and 160 crew members. The hull was divided into seven compartments by six watertight bulkheads. The three lower decks were made of steel and the two upper ones were built of wood.

The main dining room had a seating capacity for 276 passengers. It was located forward on the orlop deck, the lowest deck on ship, and it was finished in silvered oak with cork tile flooring. Immediately below this dining room were the stores, refrigerators, and fresh water tanks. Aft on this deck toward the rear of the ship, there was a bar which was finished in fumed oak with tile floor. The living quarters for the crew also were located on this deck.

On the main deck, the aft part of the vessel contained a large social hall and the passenger entrance. Aft, adjacent to the social hall there was the purser's room, the barber shop, the cafe, and the parcel check room. Forward from the social hall there was the baggage room and the living accommodations for the engineering crew. The galley was located on the main deck amidship. A series of elevators and dumb waiters connected the galley with the pantry and storerooms below. Forward from the galley there was the lower cabin which was surrounded by nine parlor staterooms, each with private bath and fitted with double brass beds and mahogany furniture. The main salon on this deck was reached from the social hall below, by the main stairway. This salon was finished in cream enamel and leading away from it were 128 staterooms with accommodations for 256 passengers. Next to the main salon, and separated by a glassed partition and French doors, the ladies' cabin was finished in silvered oak. Both the main salon and the ladies' cabin were furnished with leather chairs and small, comfortable sofas. The promenade deck contained 52 staterooms and 14 parlor staterooms with baths. An outdoor, covered promenade, nine feet wide and lined with deck and steamer chairs, encircled the ship. The extreme aft of this deck included a children's open air playground, and was supplied with all sorts of toys. Swings, hammocks, and a pile of pure white sand also attracted the youngsters. The railing around this area was completely screened in with wire netting to prevent accidents.

On the boat deck there were 57 more staterooms and eight more parlor staterooms. The Captain's quarters were located at the forward end of the boat deck directly under the pilot-house. At the extreme aft end of the boat deck there was a glass-enclosed ballroom which was fitted with a hardwood maple floor for dancing. Lights throughout the ship were powered by electricity, and all rooms were cooled by mechanical air conditioning, for which a 12-ton refrigeration unit was installed. All water used for washing, bathing, or drinking was filtered.

SOUTH AMERICAN

A topside view of the *South American.* Photo by Harry J. Wolf.

No sooner it seemed, had the *North* and *South American* begun pleasing their customers, when the death of Robert Davis in 1916, placed the firm on the brink of financial disaster. The economic problems of World War I further compounded this crisis, but these were only temporary setbacks in the company's progress, and following the war, the customers returned, along with financial stability. In 1922, both ships were converted to run on oil fuel, and each received a second smokestack. The old stacks on each ship were also cut down and slanted slightly to match the size and design of the new stacks.

The years that followed were happy ones filled with sunshine memories and moonlit romances that stood for the very essence of the *South American.* But life for this ship and for her passengers was not always calm and peaceful. One shocking and tragic incident in which the vessel was involved happened during the early morning hours of September 9, 1924. A crew of 16 men was laying up the vessel for winter after she had drydocked at Holland, Michigan five days before. A fire, said to have been ignited by a cigarette smouldering in some stored linen, completely gutted and destroyed the ship. The fire started amidship near the engine room, where 560 gallons of fuel oil had been stored. Once the fire reached that oil, there were a number of violent explosions which tore out large sections of her hull and endangered the lives of the firemen who were fighting to contain the blaze. Several summer cottages nearby were ignited by flying embers from the fire and a warehouse at the scene also was badly damaged.

Representatives of the Georgian Bay line stated that the vessel, then 10 years old, would cost $1,250,000 to replace. The vessel had been originally built at a cost of $600,000. The work soon commenced, and what was even more astonishing than the cost, was the fact that the *South American* was completely remodeled at Ecorse and ready for her cruises by June, the following year. Her spring passengers remarked "that you could never tell there had been a fire."

Another dramatic event took place during her later years on a run to Buffalo. Captain Harold Nelson was trying to make the breakwall outside Buffalo in the face of stiff 40 knot west winds and a mean following sea. Just moments away from docking and safe from the rapidly deteriorating weather conditions, the Coast Guard radioed Captain Nelson with orders not to enter the breakwall! Because of the high seas, there was too little water in the sea trough, the long, narrow hollow between the waves, and the ship would surely go aground. Captain Nelson had but a few seconds to make a decision of hard right or hard left. Left was his choice, but even with the quick action taken, the *South American* almost floundered. Caught in the trough, she went into a severe starboard list with the winds literally pushing her over. She felt as though she would never come up. Chaos and pandemonium turned fear stricken passengers and crew topsy-turvy as everything not securely tied down was sliding all over the place. Dinner was being prepared at that moment and all of it ended up in a scrambled mess. Luggage slipped from secure places, and Chief Engineer Bill Bates was standing on the side of the engine

Above, this egg timer trinket was once sold to passengers on the *South American.* The highball glass shows the insignia of the Georgian Bay Line.

58

The interior view of the ship above, reflects the elaborate decor which characterized this beautiful lady. Photo by Harry J. Wolf. Left, this souvenir plate also was sold aboard ship.

Top right, a passenger prepares to say "Bon voyage." Photo by Harry J. Wolf. Right, an early photo of the *South American* before she acquired her second smokestack in 1922. Photo courtesy William Hayward collection. Opposite, a view of her stern. Photo by Harry J. Wolf.

awaiting sure disaster. Ever so gradually, however, the ship righted herself and continued on around the north shore of Lake Erie to the nearest port which was at Port Colborne, Ontario. It meant going some 20 miles farther, but most of that time was spent cleaning up the mess and calming down the passengers.

With the advent of the modern freeway system to speed automobile travel, and with the increase in the amount of airplane travel as well, the declining years of the Great Lakes excursion vessels were well under way, but the *South American* seemed to be holding her own. In spite of a few changes in management and in seeing her business suffer during the war periods, she was still going strong in 1958 when she added several more bright stars to her career record.

By virtue of being the first passenger vessel to travel through the new portion of the St. Lawrence Seaway, she established several notable firsts: She was the first vessel to use the new Iroquois, Eisenhower, and Snell locks; she was the first vessel with more than a 14-foot draft to transit the new Seaway locks; and she was the first vessel with more than a 14-foot draft to navigate the St. Lawrence River from Clayton to Massena, New York. In 1967, she made 18 scheduled trips through the Seaway, carrying an estimated 10,000 passengers to Montreal for Expo 67.

But the era of the beautiful *"Sweetheart South"* was over. She was sold to the Seafarers International Union for $111,111.11 immediately after her Expo cruises to replace her sister ship the *North American,* which had mysteriously gone down in some 220 feet of water in the Atlantic off Nantucket, Massachusetts in September, 1967.

Thus departing Detroit for the last time on October 16, 1967, under her own power, she headed for Montreal and a short time later was towed to Newport News, Virginia where her engines were removed. The liquidation of the Georgian Bay Line soon followed, chiefly because the company was unsuccessful in its attempt to secure a replacement vessel for the *South American.*

When several attempts to turn the *South American* into a training ship school at Piney Point, Maryland failed, the Seafarers International Union sold her for scrap. Since that time there have been numerous efforts to "bring back the South," all of which have proven fruitless. The vessel now lies at the Port of South Jersey, in Camden, New Jersey. If the *South American* is truly a genuine lady, and I'm sure that she is, she certainly must feel the same sadness that many others feel by having lost their "sweetheart of the Lakes." □

Left, an interior view of the pilot house. Photo by Harry J. Wolf. Above, a life vest from the *South American.* Below, this is how the beautiful lady looked following the devastating fire at Holland, Michigan in 1924. Photo by Joe Ten Brink. And bottom, the elegant steamer now quietly rests at the Port of South Jersey in Camden, New Jersey.

GREATER DETROIT

Ships that pass in the night,
and speak each other in passing.
Only a signal shown and a
distant voice in the darkness.

Henry Wadwsorth Longfellow
"Tales of a Wayside Inn"

When the Detroit and Cleveland Navigation Company was finally disbanded in 1960, it was not destined to be soon forgotten, because their steamships had rightfully earned an honorable place alongside all of those other great ships that make up the proud maritime heritage of the Great Lakes. For over 100 years, its ships had plied the Great Lakes, providing both passengers and area residents with far more than a simple and economical means of transportation, as well as a spectacular view from the shore. To their faithful patrons, the D & C steamships had provided them with a romantic means of travel that could not be readily duplicated by road or by rail. Many years later, former passengers would nostalgically recall those moonlit nights with the soft winds gently blowing across the lake, peaceful nights whose stillness was broken only by the bow of the ship slicing through calm waters. To the local residents, the passing ships and their haunting whistles beckoned them irresistibly with a siren's song from Memorial Day to Labor Day, and these people would fondly remember how eagerly they awaited the first warm breezes of spring because it promised the return of their old friends and the passage of those ships that had become legends.

In 1922, the owners of the proud D & C Line envisioned a dream of offering elegant but affordable nightly transportation in the Great Lakes area on a scale that had not been previously achieved. With noted marine architect Frank Kirby to design their fleet of ships, the D & C owners saw their dream become a reality when the *Greater Detroit* and her sister ship the *Greater Buffalo* were both completed in the summer of 1924. Proudly, the *Greater Detroit* sailed into the harbor at Buffalo, New York on her maiden voyage the morning of August 29th, a route she would follow countless times over the next three decades. And it was obvious from the warm reception that awaited her, that she was going to be well received by the public, because those people who lined the shore greeted her enthusiastically with much fanfare and flag-waving, band playing and applause. Members of Buffalo's fire and police departments even formed an honor guard to help her launch a career that would last for 32 years. Even those people who had turned out on that August morning simply out of curiosity to see this brand new ship that was the "talk of the town" were not disappointed. The largest sidewheeler ever built in the world was indeed an awe-inspiring sight as she glided towards the dock. Her massiveness was overwhelming, especially for a Great Lakes passenger vessel! With a length of 535 feet, a beam of 58 feet, 3 inches, and a gross tonnage of 7,739 tons, she was able to easily attain speeds of up to 21 miles per hour. She carried a crew of 300 including officers, but she could sail with a minimum crew of 175, if her load were light. She also was able to transport 2,127 passengers and she could carry 130 automobiles in her hold.

This gigantic vessel truly fulfilled her owners' expectations. Costing $3,500,000 to construct, the *Greater Detroit* was without question an elegant ship. She contained grand appointments that could be enjoyed by all who boarded her, regardless of their financial status or social position. And yet, within the rich atmosphere of the ship, a feeling of airiness and spaciousness prevailed. Her architectural features were an experience to behold. Elaborate main ceiling arches which stretched upward for three stories highlighted the main salon which was fashioned in the classic style of the Italian Renaissance. Touches of the finest wood were apparent everywhere on the liner, from the stylishly paneled promenade deck to the mahogany beamed ceilings found in some of her rooms. Even the stairwells were graced with ornate, curved banisters. Many original oil paintings and murals, depicting various historic scenes pertaining to the Great Lakes were located at several vantage points throughout the vessel. One of these works, the "Battle of Lake Erie, Sept. 10, 1813," was particularly meaningful to passengers of the *Greater Detroit*, because their journey would frequently carry them over the very same waters of that historic confrontation.

Because of the ship's attractive decor, one might have expected that it would have been very expensive to travel on one of her cruises. To the contrary, however, fares were quite reasonable and within the financial reach of most people. For as little as $3.75, for example, one could obtain passage from Detroit to Buffalo, and for a mere $3.50 more, that same passenger could secure an inside room where he or she could rest or relax for the entire trip if desired.

No class distinction was made aboard the *Greater Detroit*, but her staterooms did offer varying degrees of luxury. While the 650 basic staterooms provided running water, an additional 130 staterooms also contained toilets, and there were 26 parlors, the most elegant of accommodations, which also contained private connecting baths. Each of these suites, located on both the promenade and galley decks, included twin beds, chairs, a sofa, a desk and a night table. Some of the parlors even had private balconies which provided the occupants

Above, a passenger baggage token from the D & C steamer *Greater Detroit.*

GREATER DETROIT

an unobstructed view of the water and passing skylines. And in equally elaborate and comfortable surroundings, the ship also had a dining room capacity of nearly 400.

For three decades, the *Greater Detroit* faithfully ferried passengers and cargo between Detroit and Buffalo. By no means was this her only responsibility, however, for occasionally she was available for charter runs. On hot summer nights, for example, she might carry a lively convention of businessmen into the upper lakes or on a quiet and pleasant Sunday afternoon she might take a church group on a ship-board picnic.

The D & C Line also offered special graduation cruises that would take groups of enthusiastic high school seniors on an unforgettable class trip. But such trips were not simply a few hours of cruising the bay. Oh no, they were complete three and four day cruises to such romantic places as Niagara Falls or Mackinac Island. A full itinerary of fun-filled activities was planned for each cruise. In addition to the sightseeing trips scheduled at their final destination, some of the activities on board ship included dancing, treasure hunts, talent shows, community sing-alongs, contests, and a number of deck games. Shuffleboard, of course, was always the overwhelming favorite. The D & C Line would offer some 15 different cruises each

Above, passengers enjoying their Great Lakes cruise on the sun deck, and this notice of life-jacket instructions was posted in all staterooms.

year. Beginning around the middle of May, a typical cruise would be from Detroit to Buffalo including a special visit to Niagara Falls. This trip would take three days and the price was $26.95 per person. And this same cruise also would be offered at later dates at the end of May or in early June. Another cruise would take the students from Detroit to Sault Ste. Marie to Mackinac Island and back home to Detroit in four days. The cost of this longer trip was $32.95.

In her relatively brief history, the *Greater Detroit* had performed her duties flawlessly—she had provided elegant and economical transportation to all classes of society and she had given her passengers exciting experiences and fond memories. In retrospect, she had given her all, and she had done her very best.

Sadly, however, her best was not enough, for this glorious ship was beset by difficulties over which she had virtually no control. The *Greater Detroit* had been built in a time of the short-lived prosperity of the early 1920s, and, like so many others, her owners would soon be reeling from the shattering effects of the disastrous Depression, a financial loss from which they would never fully recover. Even more disheartening, was the realization that she belonged to an antiquated form of travel that was doomed to extinction. Following World War II, in the wake of a rapidly advancing technology, other means of

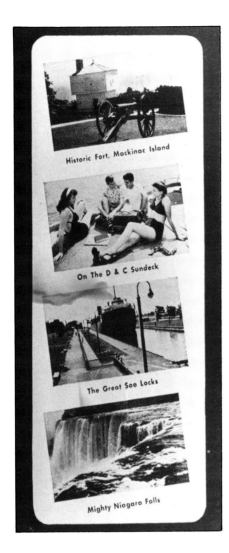

Historic Fort, Mackinac Island

On The D & C Sundeck

The Great Soo Locks

Mighty Niagara Falls

Left, a typical stateroom. Above, a preview of the ship's itinerary was found on the back of a menu. While all of the staterooms had a wall telephone, below, calls could be made only while the ship was docked. Right, a schedule for the popular graduation cruises.

D&C GRADUATION CRUISES
CLASS OF '49
Sailing Schedule

☐ **CRUISE No. 1**   **MAY 18 TO MAY 20**

From DETROIT to BUFFALO, VISITING NIAGARA FALLS and return
(You may board ship after 1:30 P.M.)

°Leave DETROIT   WEDNESDAY, MAY 18   3:00 P.M. E.S.T.

Leaving her dock your D & C Liner will head down the Detroit River and pass under the Ambassador Bridge to Lake Erie, cruising 250 miles to Buffalo. After a sumptuous dinner, a gala evening of entertainment, carnival dance, treasure hunt, with fun galore, you retire to your cabin for a restful night's sleep. Tomorrow you visit one of the seven wonders of the world — the mighty Niagara Falls. Arise and shine, early to breakfast and on deck to see your cruise liner enter the slip and dock at Buffalo, New York.

°Arrive BUFFALO   THURSDAY, MAY 19   8:00 A.M. E.S.T.

10:00 A.M. — A special train will leave N. Y. C. (Terrace Street Station) to take your party to beautiful and spectacular Niagara Falls. The Cruisers have the entire day free to explore the many points of scenic and historic interest, such as the mighty Canadian Horseshoe Falls, the American Falls, the Whirlpool Rapids, Niagara Glen, Goat Island, and time to visit the Cave of the Winds, to ride on the "Maid of the Mist", or the cable car. Students must provide their lunch on this day. The special train leaves Niagara Falls, New York, at 4:00 P.M. (E.S.T.), and once again you board your cruise ship.

°Leave BUFFALO   THURSDAY, MAY 19   6:00 P.M. E.S.T.

Homeward bound and to dinner. Then for a memorable evening of dancing, student talent show, community singing and a gala time. (PRIZES).

°Arrive DETROIT   FRIDAY, MAY 20   10:00 A.M. E.S.T.

After a hearty breakfast you say farewell to the many new-found friends and record this cruise as one of the highlights of your life.

☐ **CRUISE No. 2**   ☐ **CRUISE No. 3**
MAY 22 TO MAY 24   **JUNE 6 TO JUNE 8**

SAME ITINERARY AND EVENTS AS   SAME ITINERARY AND EVENTS AS
CRUISE NO. 1   CRUISE NO. 1

Sun.—Leave Detroit May 22 3:00 P.M. E.S.T.	Mon.—Leave Detroit June 6 3:00 P.M. E.S.T.
Mon.—Arrive Buffalo May 23 8:00 A.M. E.S.T.	Tues.—Arrive Buffalo June 7 8:00 A.M. E.S.T.
Mon.—Leave Buffalo May 23 6:00 P.M. E.S.T.	Tues.—Leave Buffalo June 7 6:00 P.M. E.S.T.
Tues.—Arrive Detroit May 24 10:00 A.M. E.S.T.	Wed.—Arrive Detroit June 8 10:00 A.M. E.S.T.

CRUISE 1-2 & 3
Price $26.95

Federal Tax $2.99 additional unless Internal Revenue Form No. 731 is used.

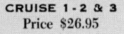

Detroit and Cleveland Navigation Co.
FOOT OF THIRD STREET — DETROIT 26, MICH.
Phone WOodward 5-0700

Late in her career, the *Greater Detroit,* was painted white, a pleasant contrast to her previous color of black.

modern transportation replaced the excursion steamship on the Great Lakes. Goods and people could be moved faster and more economically by plane, automobile, truck, or train.

So on December 12, 1956, the *Greater Detroit* was towed into Lake St. Clair, three miles out from the Grosse Pointe Yacht Club. There she was set afire so that her wooden super-structure could burn away, thus making the job of scrapping her an easier one. Thousands of saddened spectators turned out to witness the torching of this elegant lady, and even a maid who had faithfully worked aboard her for 30 years was there, with tears in her eyes.

When she burned, a romantic era had sadly come to an end. It was an era of anticipation in buying cruise tickets and in packing, making sure that nothing important would be left behind. It was an era of bustling taxis and buses dropping their excited fares off at the wharf. And it was an era of serene summer evening cruises with music softly drifting overhead and bright stars twinkling above. No longer would Great lakes residents hear the resonant bellow of her whistles or view the giant paddlewheels as they slapped methodically through the water. Now everything was quiet. As the last flame flickered and died, the *Greater Detroit* expired too, her voice extinguished forever, except in the minds of those who knew and loved her well. □

Top left, the *Greater Detroit* passes the Detroit skyline in the 1940s. That's the old Penobscot building in the middle of the photo. Center, the ship in drydock at Lorain, Ohio in 1924. Left, docked at Detroit just before her final day.

COLUMBIA

Tooooot.....tooooooot......"It's ten o'clock
and there goes the Bob-Lo boat
leaving from the foot of Woodward."

*Detroit radio commercial
of the 1960s and 1970s*

Throughout the early years of the 20th century, excursion
boating prospered and as its popularity increased, each steamship line tried to surpass its competition by providing the most
attractive, and most modern ships, along with offering the most
diverse travel itineraries and sailing schedules. Ships such as the *Put-
In-Bay, Tashmoo,* and *City of Detroit III,* were familiar, frequent sights on
the Great Lakes. By the 1950s, however, interest in excursion boating
had declined dramatically, and by the 1960s, more and more companies, faced with financial ruin, were forced to either disband their
operations altogether, or they sought to diversify their interests to
meet the needs of a rapidly changing society.

In retrospect, the rise and fall of the popularity of those recreational steamships which sailed the Great Lakes is a reflection of that
dramatic change in the character of our society which has taken place
during this century. At the turn of the century, for example, the
population of the city of Detroit was nearly 286,000, and by today's
standards, life there moved at a leisurely pace. With the bicycle and
the horse and buggy serving as the basic forms of transportation,
these people welcomed excursion boating as a natural extension of
their tranquil lifestyle. Yet, with the arrival of the automobile, and
with improved transportation, by road and by rail, rapid growth and
development were inevitable. By 1930, Detroit's population had increased sixfold and the roots of our modern society were firmly im-
planted. Although the Great Depression slowed things temporarily,
following World War II, society quickly regained its fervor for fast
living. Accelerating rapidly towards the jet age, man's desire for
speed was visible everywhere: on land, cars built with bigger engines
went faster; in the air, airplane travel superceded the railroad; and
on the water, the serene and elegant steamships also became out-
moded as speedboats and cabin cruisers supplanted them. Modern
man, now wanting to control his own recreation, dreamed of being

captain of his own ship. And for many, this dream became reality, for as the 1960s progressed, as people became more affluent than ever before, more and more people purchased their own vessels. Small pleasure craft were purchased in such great numbers, in fact, that Michigan quickly earned the distinction of having the largest number of registered pleasure craft in the United States.

With the demise of excursion liners, it would almost seem that a unique stage of maritime history had ended on the Great Lakes. To the contrary, however, one successful steamship company did not fall victim to the ill-fated destiny of other shipping companies of its era. Continuing to thrive long after all others before it failed, the Bob-Lo Company and her excursion boats have become an integral part of Detroit, moving gracefully and irreplaceably from the 1890s into the spirit of the 1980s.

The present company traces its roots to the golden age of excursion boating. In the 1890s, the Detroit, Belle Isle and Windsor Ferry Company operated a regular service that carried passengers from Detroit and Windsor to numerous local resorts and island retreats as far north as the St. Clair Flats and as far south as Belle Isle and Fighting Island. Yet realizing the need for another nearby recreation area, the owners acquired Bois Blanc Island. The French gave the island its name which means white woods because of the numerous white birch and beech trees which were found there. It was not officially recognized as Bob-Lo Island until 1908 when the owners finally conceded that most people were unable to pronounce the French words properly. Located 19 miles south of Detroit in the Canadian waters of the lower Detroit River within sight of Lake Erie, the island seemed a perfect playground for one-day outings. When the island opened in June, 1898, the company soon discovered that their observations were correct. Success came quickly as the response by church groups and businesses that scheduled annual picnics and cruises was tremendous. Within two seasons it was obvious that their original fleet of ships assigned to carry passengers to and from the island would soon be inadequate.

So in November, 1901, the company commissioned Frank Kirby to design a new vessel for them, one that would triple the capacity of their other two ships. Built by the Detroit Shipbuilding Company at its Wyandotte Yard, the *Columbia* was launched in May, 1902 and towed to the Orleans Street dock where she was completed. With three decks to accommodate her passengers, she measured 216 feet in length and had an overall breadth of 60 feet. With a draft of 12.5 feet, her gross weight was 968 tons. The new ship fulfilled all hopes, for she was able to transport 4500 people easily. Over the years, however, because marine safety standards have become more strict, the *Columbia's* capacity has gradually been diminished, and at present, she is rated to hold only 2500.

Her trial run to Bois Blanc Island on July 7, 1902 made her owners quite exuberant. With record-breaking speed, the *Columbia* reached her destination in only 80 minutes—a full 25 minutes less than either

COLUMBIA

of her predecessors! Her maiden voyage that same evening was a church-sponsored moonlight cruise. And the following day, she began her lengthy career of making regular daily runs to the island. The *Columbia* proved to be such a popular attraction during her early years of service, the company added yet another ship to the line to accommodate the great crowd who wished to visit Bois Blanc. In 1911, they commissioned the *Ste. Claire,* which was quite similar in design to the *Columbia.* Together these ships performed their duties faithfully, year in and year out, departing daily from their Woodward Avenue moorings. In 1976, when the waterfront area was renovated, the historic Bob-Lo boathouse was razed and the docks were moved west of Cobo Hall to a site once used by the boats of the Detroit and Cleveland Navigation Company.

The Detroit, Belle Isle, and Windsor Ferry Company retained their ownership for 51 years. In 1949, they sold their interest to Troy H. Browning, and for the next 30 years the Browning family worked endlessly to add, improve and develop Bob-Lo Island and the Bob-Lo boats. The Browning brothers, Ralph and William, are perhaps the most responsible for providing today's youth with the same opportunity to experience the sheer pleasure of a river cruise as their parents had, since it was during the Browning years that excursion

Although the *Columbia* was recently designated a historic vessel, she still remains as active as ever, transporting passengers to Bob-Lo Island.

Top right, the *Columbia's* sister ship, the *Ste. Claire,* leaves the old Woodward Avenue dock. That's the *City of Cleveland,* another D & C steamer in the background. Center right, a topside view of the ship. Bottom right, the Bob-Lo flag waves above the pilot house.

boating all but became extinct on the Great Lakes and they alone were able to survive. In 1979, Frank W. Donovan and the Browning family sold its control of Bob-Lo Island and the two steamers to a group of investors from Kentucky and Minnesota. For the next several years following this transaction, the company swayed in and out of bankruptcy until 1983, when the Automobile Club of Michigan bought the company and put the worries of countless Bob-Lo boat lovers to rest.

Consistently reliable throughout her many years of service, the *Columbia* has experienced a relatively quiet career. Once, however, in 1905, she did run aground at Peche Island when she was on a moonlight cruise. Fortunately, there was no damage and most of her passengers actually seemed to enjoy their all-night delay, making the best of it by dancing the night away under the stars until they were rescued by another ship the next morning. And there must have been a great deal of excitement on that day in 1923 when a baby girl was born aboard the *Columbia*.

Captain Linwood R. Beattie has been at her helm since about 1944. He came to the *Columbia* with proven experience, for he had sailed for the Navy in World War II and also had served a term as a deep sea tug captain. His expertise in handling the old girl is widely acclaimed and it is said that Captain Beattie knows her so well, he can direct her on to a lily pad.

As an undeniable tribute to her glory, the *Columbia* was recently declared a historic vessel; yet she remains as active as ever. Every

Above, Captain Bob-Lo, the symbolic goodwill ambassador of the Bob-Lo boats who greeted passengers for more than 70 years. Photo courtesy Dossin Great Lakes Museum Collection.

Ferrying people to and from Bob-Lo Island on numerous trips daily, little has changed for the *Columbia* in her nearly 80 years of service.

summer from May until September, she and the *Ste. Claire* maintain busy schedules, ferrying people to and from Bob-Lo on numerous trips daily. On weekends, those venerable ladies cruise the waters on romantic, moonlight voyages, creating special magic for all who are on board. During the 1960s, the Bob-Lo boats began making two special cruises northward, one on the Fourth of July and the other on Labor Day. Especially memorable, was the Labor Day cruise which took passengers to Port Huron amidst much festivity. During the ship's passage up the St. Clair River, crowds along the shore met her enthusiastically, shouting greetings, waving flags, releasing balloons, and even firing cannons. A new dimension was later added as she passed the River Crab restaurant in St. Clair. There the *Columbia* paused to exchange salutes with many of the old steam whistles which had been brought there for the annual whistle blowing contest. What an unforgettable experience for those lucky enough to be aboard her on that day, as the present was merged subtly with the past. And how easy it must have been for the participants to imagine the ghosts of ships long deceased as the *Columbia* retraced the very course of her lofty ancestors, receiving the same fanfare that awaited them so long ago.

Possibly this is why the Bob-Lo boats have endured. For no matter when they sail, those beloved steamers weave a spell of enchantment for all who board them. In truth, how little has actually changed in the nearly 80 years from *Columbia's* first sailing. Then, a small child often approached the gangplank with great reluctance, overwhelmed by the enormous size of the ship and the undertaking at hand. Often-times a band would play on the docks and the child might feel as though he or she were beginning an ocean voyage. Today, although no band greets the embarking passengers, a small child may still approach the gangplank apprehensively, still wide-eyed and glowing! And when the whistle bellows to signify departure, it resounds with the sacred promise of a fun-filled day. There is barely a passenger, child or adult, who can remain untouched by such eagerness and enthusiasm. And who could ever forget the adorable midget, Captain Bob-Lo, the longtime symbolic ambassador of goodwill of the Bob-Lo excursions, who most people believed was actually the captain of the ship. It was this familiar figure who was often there to greet the new arrivals, especially to calm the fears of the young ones who were about to come aboard.

Today, as in years gone by, within an hour-and-a-half the boat reaches her destination at that same small island lodged snugly at the gateway to Lake Erie. When passengers alight, troubles and age seem to disappear simultaneously, as father and son, mother and daughter share equally the thrill of the roller coaster and the excitement of the Pirate's Ship. Time passes all too quickly, for once again the whistle of the stalwart *Columbia* bellows, calling all eternal youth back to reality. On the return voyage home, that pleasurable glow may still flicker, but then it must be wistfully extinquished, carefully tucked away until yet another summer arrives.　　　　　　□

DAVID DOWS

A wet sheet and a flowing sea,
A wind that follows fast
And fills the white and rustling sail
And bends the gallant mast.

Allan Cunningham
"A Wet Sheet and a Flowing Sea"

The maritime history of the Great Lakes has essentially focused on two types of ships—those used for pleasure, and those used for commerce. In the preceeding chapters, you've read about several of those wonderful excursion boats and how they brought so much pleasure to so many people during the first half of this century. But historically, those other ships, the early freighters and the lumber schooners for example, have played a much more significant role by first transporting countless numbers of westward moving pioneers to settle in Michigan, the midwest, and beyond, and later by carrying much of the freight necessary to build the cities and towns populated by those immigrants. Today, of course, the big ore boats dominate the scene. But during the 19th Century, a time of extensive territorial expansion, masses of hardy settlers expedited their arduous treks westward by journeying over water rather than on land. Sailing from Buffalo, New York, most would leave ship in Detroit and proceed from there into the interior, but many would also sail on, around the Lower Peninsula, to ports along the southern shores of Lake Michigan. In terms of commerce, merchants were well aware of the beneficial aspects of the lakes and hastened to capitalize on them. First, as a connecting link between major ports, water routes eliminated the time, the expense, and the difficulty of transporting goods over land. Secondly, these ships could carry an almost limitless variety of commercial cargo. Grain, meat, minerals, and even whiskey were among the valuable commodities stored in the holds of these ships. At this time too, a merchant could select either a steamship or a sailing vessel to transport his wares. But while steamships were gradually replacing sailing craft as commercial vehicles in the last half of the 1800s, sailing vessels nonetheless retained their importance to commercial enterprises, and continued to be profitable. Among the latter type of sailing craft, one ship surpassed all others with respect to magnificence and size. She was the world's first five masted schooner and she also was the only one to ever sail the Great Lakes. She was the grand ship *David Dows.*

The unique idea for a five masted schooner was conceived in the spring of 1880 by the Toledo firm of Carrington and Casey, a prominent merchant ship company. To make their dream a reality, the firm contracted the Bailey brothers to build the *David Dows* in their shipyard on the banks of the Maumee River. More than 100 able craftsmen took part, using no less than the finest quality materials, including, as the story goes, "a grove of stately oaks," to fashion the ship's exquisite lines. Their workmanship produced a fine vessel that was truly exceptional indeed. Her regal silhouette was an imposing one that commanded immediate attention, and her accommodations were the finest of any merchant ship. Thus there was little doubt in anyone's mind that she was a special ship as the large crowd of curious onlookers gathered on that memorable day in May of 1881 to observe the start of her maiden voyage.

Although commonly referred to as a schooner, the *David Dows* was actually a five-masted barkentine having square sails on the foremast, and fore and aft sails on the remaining masts. Her long black hull and soaring masts were awe inspiring. The hull measured 265 feet four inches in length, and the 37 foot, 6 inch beam supported five majestic masts, ranging in diameter from 21 to 36 inches at their base. These towering "sticks" going aft, were 93 feet, 97 feet, 97 feet, 93 feet, and 88 feet high. All of the topmasts measured another 65 feet, except the jigger-topmast, which was 55 feet. In other words, her tallest mast reached an incredible height of 162 feet. In addition, the square rigged foremast contained two topsails, and two topgallant sails above those. This lofty aerial framework thus carried some 70,000 yards of the finest Mt. Vernon duck canvas, which was enough fabric, according to the April 21, 1881 edition of the Toledo *Blade,* "to furnish clean shirts for a large portion of the Democratic party in Ohio." Not too surprisingly, a steam donkey engine was utilized to raise these billowing sheets, and even then, it took her 12-man crew anywhere between four and eight hours to complete the task of hoisting sail and coiling down. The *David Dows* also was reported to have had a carved figurehead, although such decorations were virtually non-existent on Great Lakes vessels. Unlike the romantic clipper ships which sailed the oceans, the schooners of the Great Lakes were essentially work ships and thus they were not usually given such elaborate features. But the glorious *Dows* was an exception. Representing the image of a dragon, her reportedly beautiful figurehead was carved by G. H. Buck, a fine craftsman from Buffalo.

The interior construction of the schooner reflected the same professional character that was exhibited by her appearance. Touring the ship for the first time, guests were amazed to find the furnishings and appointments no less luxurious than those of the finest hotels of the period. The forecastle which was above deck contained berths for eight crew members and provided them with a cozy sitting room. The cabin also above deck housed the officers and included an attrac-

DAVID DOWS

tive dining room. This room was decorated with hand carved ceiling panels and rich wood grained doors. The galley boasted marble-topped wash basins, while the store room amidships contained a refrigerator, quite an innovative and modern convenience which permitted the cook to keep meat and ice for longer periods of time while the ship was under way.

But the *David Dows* was primarily intended to carry commerical cargo and for this she was appropriately designed. Eight large hatches aboard her decks made loading easier and faster. The hold itself was yet another example of expertise and solid workmanship, as the heavy oak walls were beautifully crafted, finely fitted, and skillfully joined together. Although these storage areas would normally contain 2500 to 2800 tons of soft coal or 90,000 bushels of wheat, they were capable of containing even greater loads. Regrettably, the *Dows* never carried her full cargo capacity, because the shallow waters of the lake harbors at that time, made it impossible for her to do so.

Her striking features and her merits as a commercial transport enabled the *David Dows* to earn the respect and affection of many. And while many of these followers were casual observers, some of her strongest advocates were found among those who sailed her. Specifically, her greatest admirer was her captain, Joseph Leonard Skeldon, an earnest seaman and a most able sailor who was deeply committed to his ship. Voluntarily, he assumed full responsibility for the ship before she was launched and he closely supervised every detail of her construction in the shipyard. No captain could ever love a ship more than Captain Skeldon loved the *Dows,* and he continued to express that love and devotion in the later years of his life as he spent many hours making highly detailed models of the schooner.

Far from being a passive individual, however, Captain Skeldon was a competitive master who actively and eagerly sought adventure, and frequently used his skill to further the accomplishments of the *David Dows.* In one voyage from Buffalo to Toledo, for example, the huge schooner completed the trip in 18 hours. This new record was indeed a great accomplishment, especially in view of the fact that

Above, the author's first rendition of the five-masted schooner *David Dows.*

OPERATED BY
UNION RAILROAD ELEVATOR COMPANY.

For many years the photo above right, was believed to be the only one ever taken of the ship. Courtesy Great Lakes Historical Society Collection. Center right, the *Dows* is featured on this advertising poster for the Union Railroad Elevator Company. Right, an early painting of the ship courtesy Great Lakes Historical Society.

many *steamers* that followed the identical route were unable to complete the trip in the same amount of time.

Further evidence of the captain's competitive nature was found in a friendly rivalry that existed between Skeldon and another competent seaman and ship's captain, who happened also to be Skeldon's brother-in-law. According to Mrs. Paul Allen Leidy, Captain Skeldon's granddaughter, whenever the two men were headed for the same port, Captain Joe always reached his destination first. Being a fair-minded and good-natured person, however, Skeldon agreed to put his reputation on the line once more to determine once and for all whether his string of victories was the result of his own ability, or was simply because he had the faster ship. Amid much speculation about who would be the ultimate victor, the confident participants exchanged ships! In an exciting race, the controversy was finally resolved as Captain Joe repeated his earlier success and finished first, much to the chagrin of his disenchanted opponent.

Joseph Skeldon navigated the dignified and graceful *David Dows* for the majority of her existence and theoretically, you might assume that the combination of his skill as a captain and her attributes as a fine ship would have made the *Dows* an unparalled success. In reality, however, her short career was a difficult one, often marked by adversity and marred by misfortune. Ominously, she was beset with troubles even before she was launched. On February 17, 1881, while the ship was under construction, one of the worst floods to ever occur on the Maumee River threatened her very existence. No one understood more clearly the peril that loomed over the *Dows* than those dedicated workmen who had watched this great ship grow right before their eyes. As many of the workers stood silently, yet anxiously, on the shore with their eyes riveted to the dark, raging flood waters, each man knew full well that those men on board would have to act quickly to avoid the tragic consequences—the ship was on the verge of floating away! And more than a few breathed a loud sigh of relief as the crew completed a risky but successful manuever to scuttle the ship, but in doing so saved her from inevitable destruction. Several days after the flood waters subsided, the ship was refloated once again, and her construction was resumed.

Near the close of her first profitable season, the *David Dows*, met with her second catastrophe, a controversial incident that occurred on Lake Erie. On the night of September 10, 1881, three vessels were bound for Buffalo. Sailing eastward on parallel courses, a little more than half-a-mile apart, the *David Dows* sailed on the north side of the formation, with the three masted schooner *Charles K. Nims* in the middle, and the schooner *John B. Merrill* on the south side. Around 8 o'clock the wind shifted direction and a sudden gust caused the ships to alter their positions. While the *Nims* was able to recover her original heading eastward, the *Dows* had changed her course to the south. In this position, the outcome was inescapable and the *Dows* ran down and sank the *Nims*. And although it was fortunate that no lives were lost, allegations and accusations were vehemently levelled by

Above, the only other known photo of the *David Dows* courtesy M. J. Brown collection. Right, Captain Joseph Skeldon, once master of the ship. Photo courtesy Mrs. Paul Allen Leidy. Opposite, an early drawing of the *Dows* that was first published in 1883. Courtesy C. E. Stein collection.

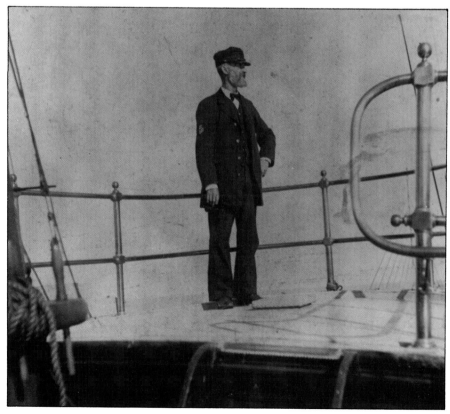

both parties, each blaming the other, but the official ruling from a later hearing on the matter declared that both ships shared responsibility for the accident.

Some time later the *David Dows* was involved in another collision, but this time the results were far more tragic. In this case, the *Dows* had struck the schooner *Richard Mott* in Lake Michigan. When the collision occurred, four men were aloft furling sail on the *Mott.* The impact caused the mast to snap and the men were thrown to their deaths. Following this accident, the *Dows* was relieved of her topmasts. It was said that she could not be handled properly with any number of men, and that her construction had been a mistake. She was called uncontrollable and dangerous, and so she was thus demoted from the ranks of being a first class merchant ship. From that point on she usually assumed the lowly guise of a tow barge.

The schooner worked in this capacity until final disaster struck in late November, 1889. Sailing from Erie, Pennsylvania, she was heading for Chicago, carrying a load of coal. As she reached the top of the lakes, she was picked up by the tug *Aurora.* The fact that she sailed under her own power supports the theory that she did have a figurehead. Although she had been stripped down to serve as a barge, she still had her sails, and so it is unlikely that her figurehead would have been removed because it was considered a good luck charm. As the two ships reached southern Lake Michigan, just off Whiting, Indiana, on November 28, the cold and windy day was typical for that time of year, and as the weather grew worse as the day progressed, strong gale force winds began battering both ships. The *Dows* had sprung a leak and water was rapidly filling her hold.

This model of the schooner *David Dows* above, was made by H. Nissley. Above right, the author's rendition of how the *Dows* figurehead may have looked. Center right, a drawing by the author of the *Dows* at Collinwood, Ontario.

Fearing that she would sink, her tow line was released and she was placed at anchor. The *Dows* struggled valiantly for some time under the great force of the wind and the waves. Then, to make matters worse, her donkey engine which had been operating the pumps, gave out. Now completely water-logged and awash, her crew took to the rigging where they were rescued several hours later by the tug *Chicago*. Each man from the *Dows* was thoroughly exhausted from the ordeal, and several of them had suffered frostbite. The next morning, a wrecking crew sailed out to the *Dows* to investigate the chances of saving her, but they found the ship so covered with ice that it was impossible to even heave up or slip her anchors. All agreed that any hope of saving the *Dows* was fruitless and the men immediately left the vessel in fear of going down with her. No sooner had they left the ship when suddenly the *Dows* gave a heavy lurch to port and sank in 30 to 36 feet of water. As she settled in her final resting place, she righted on her keel so that all of her five masts were showing above the water. And so, this once proud ship, in less than a decade after her promising career had begun, succumbed to those very same elements which have claimed so many other ships on the Great Lakes throughout history. But for the *David Dows*, although she suffered the same fate as those other ships, she will always be remembered as the giant of the Great Lakes sailing ships. □

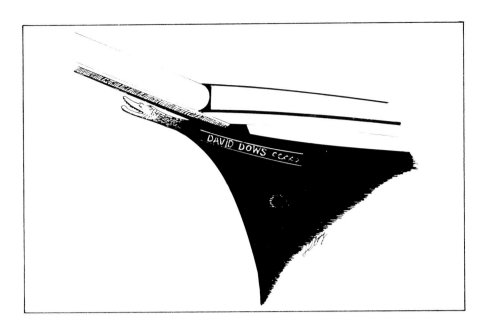

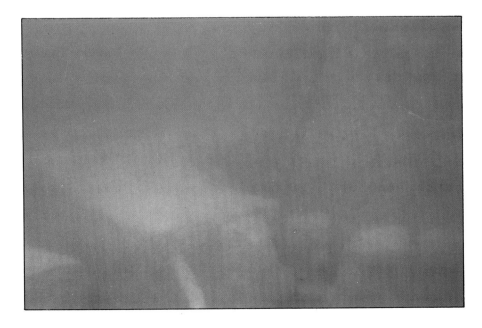

There is, however, a special footnote to the saga of the *David Dows*. In 1978, a group of divers headed by David Groover of Grand Rapids, Michigan, under the author's direction performed an investigative dive on the wreck of the *Dows* in lower Lake Michigan. Because the *Dows* was one of only a few Great Lakes ships to have carried a figurehead, the team of divers intended to recover this rare artifact, under state permit, for placement in a Great Lakes museum. However, after two days, the divers determined that the area above the figurehead was covered with deep sand. While this development halted the recovery, further attempts are still pending. Left, an underwater photo of the *Dows* rudder post as it lies on the bottom of Lake Michigan. Photo by David Groover.

LUCIA A. SIMPSON

Majestic woods of ev'ry vigorous green,
Stage above stage, high waving o'er the hills,
Or to the far horizon wide diffused,
A boundless deep immensity of shade.

Thomson

At the peak of Michigan's great logging era, immense areas of timberland were harvested to satisfy the needs of the growing West. Not only had Michigan pine built Chicago, for example, the state's forests also very quickly provided the huge quantities of pine that rebuilt that city after the great fire in 1871. Within four years following that catastrophe, visitors said they could find little to indicate that Chicago was ever touched by fire. And in 1884, more than 8,000 cargoes of cedar shingles, and pine lumber of all shapes and sizes were shipped to Chicago to make cities out of other towns throughout the Midwest. The peak was reached in 1890 when five and one-half billion board feet of Michigan lumber were cut. After this immense effort, Michigan began to slip slowly from prominence, so that by 1900, although Michigan was still a leader in lumber production, the end was in sight.

During this lumbering heyday, the construction of the distinctive Great Lakes schooner also reached an all time high, as more than 1700 schooners plied the Great Lakes from 1870 to 1900, heavily laden with the trade of the times. Many of these vessels carried an unusual triangular sail on the foremast, called the raffee. This particular sail, first introduced on the Great Lakes, could be manned by fewer men and was easier to handle. The schooners also were fitted with centerboards, a keel-like device that could be raised and lowered through a water-tight box inside the vessel, to allow the ship to be more easily maneuvered when moving in a windward direction. And because their ships were required to travel through narrow harbors and rivers, their flat-sided hulls had less beam and were longer than their ocean-going counterparts.

The three-masted schooner *Lucia A. Simpson* was typical of the lumber ships of her time, but she had the proud distinction of being one of the last schooners to sail on Lake Michigan. The *Simpson* was built at Manitowoc, Wisconsin at the Rand and Burger yards in 1875.

She measured 127 feet long, had a beam of 28 feet, and her mainmast stood 117 feet above her deck.

Through the great lumbering era and beyond, the *Simpson* continued her active career until she was replaced by the larger steam cargo vessels which arrived on the Great Lakes through the newly enlarged locks and canals which connected the lakes with the Atlantic Ocean. With these inevitable advancements came larger cargoes and more efficient operations. And within a short period of time, the graceful schooners were left idle alongside the road to progress. By 1910, there were but a handful of actual sailing ships still in service, and a number of those were being towed as barges. Among them, the *Simpson* found work and cargo until 1929, when, while making a trip north, she was hit by a squall off Algoma in Lake Michigan. She lost her mizzen mast and she began to take on water through the well worn seams in her hull. Working feverishly at the pumps, her captain and crew managed to save the 54-year-old ship.

She was towed to Sturgeon Bay to be repaired, but because of the major expenses that would be involved, repair was deemed out of the question. Then in 1934, Manitowoc city officials considered buying the vessel to make her a floating museum. But before the project was fully implemented, a fire at the Sturgeon Bay yards destroyed the *Simpson*.

And thus, sailing into the twilight of one of the most fascinating eras of Great Lakes maritime history, the *Lucia A. Simpson* will long serve as a cherished memory of the grace and romance of the golden age of the grand sailing ships. □

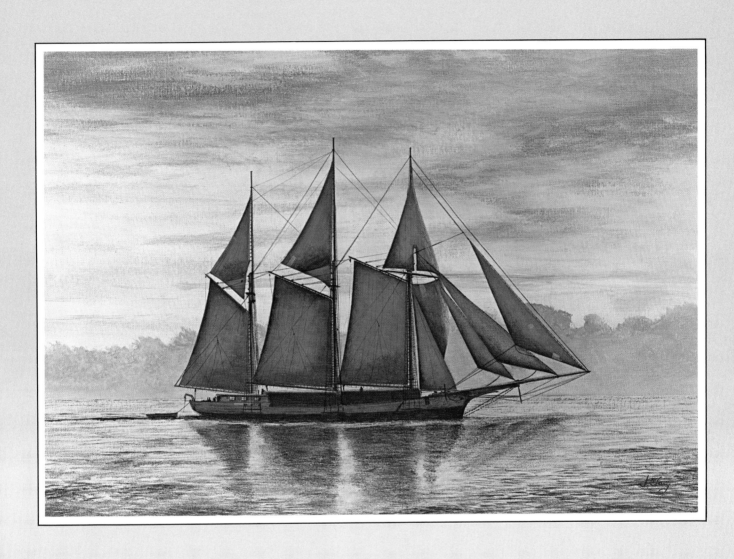

LUCIA A. SIMPSON

The *Lucia A. Simpson* in port. Courtesy Manitowoc Maritime Museum Collection.

Above, a close-up view of the deck of the lumber schooner *Lucia A. Simpson*. Photo courtesy Manitowoc Maritime Museum Collection. Right, a photo of the schooner broadside under full sail with a large load of lumber.

A rare photo of the tug *Goldsmith* above, pulling six schooners near Sturgeon Bay, Wisconsin in 1892. Left, this model of the *Simpson* in a 1000 watt light bulb was made by Steve Vickery.

U.S.S. MICHIGAN

A song of strength and a song of speed,
Of the dream made true and the word made deed,
In bow and bulwarks and ribs and keel,
An epic in iron, an ode in steel.

Unknown

W
hile most of the ships to sail the inland seas were either
recreational or commercial vessels, not all lake traffic has
been restricted to those two categories. Throughout
history, some of the other vessels which have plied the waves have
been military craft whose presence has ensured tranquility and has
maintained harmony on the Great Lakes. Among these craft, the
United States Ship Michigan was one of the most famous. The Navy's
first iron-hulled ship, the *U.S.S. Michigan* also was one of the few
armed Great Lakes vessels to never fire its guns in combat.

Authorized by Congress in 1842, the *U.S.S. Michigan* had been
built, launched, and commissioned at Erie, Pennsylvania in less than
two years time, and by the termination of her service in 1923, 39 different officers had served as her captain. A full crew usually consisted
of 106 men and they skillfully manned this uniquely, yet solidly built
ship. With a length of 163 feet, a beam of 27 feet, and a draft of nine
feet when fully loaded, her displacement exceeded 680 tons. She was
rigged as a barkentine, a three masted ship, and her wooden super-
structure rested on her iron hull while two wooden paddle wheels
and two steam engines along with her sails were used for propulsion.

Her extraordinary construction was truly a source of amazement
to all observers and a vigilant crowd had gathered to witness
her launching in December, 1843. As launch time approached,
speculation mounted, for although her loyal supporters displayed
unabashed confidence in her superiority, some opinionated critics
scoffed, equally certain that a ship made of heavy iron would never
float! Amid growing tension, the *U.S.S. Michigan* began to slide down
the ways towards the waiting waters of Lake Erie. However, before
she could make the final plunge, the ship became stuck on the ways
and her journey came to an abrupt halt. Numerous attempts were
made to get her moving again but all of them failed, and finally in
disappointment, the crowd of curiosity seekers and well wishers

dispersed. Not to be defeated, the shipyard workers returned the next morning determined to complete the launch. To their complete surprise, however, they discovered that the pride of the Navy, in a burst of independence perhaps, had launched herself! Buoyant upon the waves, she proudly flaunted her seaworthiness and totally disproved the bleak predictions of those skeptics who thought she would sink under her own weight.

Now that she had been successfully launched, the next stage of construction was carefully carried out. Systematically, the ship was fully outfitted with sail and rigging until she was adequately equipped to fulfill her duties as a warship. Next, four 32 pound carronades and two 68 pound Paixhans guns were brought on board and placed in position. Unfortunately, when the Navy had initially requisitioned this armament it had inadvertently overlooked the stipulations of the Rush-Bagot Gentleman's Agreement of 1817, an agreement between the United States and Great Britian which limited the size and the number of warships that could sail on the Great Lakes, and which also restricted the munitions for each ship to a single 18 pound cannon. Upon hearing that the United States had just launched a new warship for the Great Lakes, Great Britain dispatched one of its diplomats to inspect the ship. Imagine his horror when he saw all of the heavy artillery on board. Knowledgeable about the provisions of the aforementioned agreement, however, the diplomat immediately lodged a formal complaint with the government. Once informed about the discrepancy by embarrassed officials in Washington, the Navy reluctantly removed all of the armament, and replaced it with the acceptable single 18 pound cannon. But her long years of service would prove that any argument about her munitions was really quite unnecessary because during her lifetime, the U.S.S. Michigan would never fire its gun in either aggression or defense!

Nevertheless, the career of the U.S.S. Michigan was far from a quiet one and her history included a great diversity of experiences. Although serenity dominated her latter years of service, a flourish of exciting activity punctuated her early years. Between 1851 and 1866, four separate incidents occurred which either involved her in political activism and violence or entangled her in espionage and intrigue. The first incident occurred in the spring of 1851. At this time, a large colony of Mormons led by James Jesse Strang lived on Beaver Island in Lake Michigan. Strang's followers had begun to settle there four years previously, arriving in small groups from Voree, Wisconsin where the main community had been established in 1844. The Mormon church had been established by Joseph Smith in New York in 1830, but continuously harassed and persecuted wherever they went, the Mormons were forced to move westward, first to Ohio, then to Missouri, and then to Illinois. It was there in February, 1844, that James Jesse Strang became a Mormon. Smith performed the baptism himself and at Strang's request, this newly appointed Elder of the church was given permission to establish the colony in Wisconsin. Then on June 27, 1844, Smith was murdered, and a fight for control

U.S.S. MICHIGAN

An early photo of the *Michigan* above, prior to her refitting in 1905. Left, this eagle carving decorated one of the two paddle wheel housings on the ship. Both photos courtesy Erie County Historical Society.

of the church quickly followed. While a few Mormons followed Strang, Brigham Young eventually emerged as the new leader of the church. About a year later, Strang claimed to have received a message from God that told him to move the colony to a "land amidst wide waters and covered with large timber with a deep, broad bay on one side of it." Strang personally selected Beaver Island. By 1850 the Mormon community on Beaver Island was thriving. But there was also growing opposition from other residents throughout northern Michigan who felt threatened by their presence. Strang then held a church meeting in July of that year where he introduced a new revelation which designated that Strang be crowned "King." His staged "coronation" strengthened his control over the colony, but it also gave those opposed to Strang more reason to hate him.

Strang's political influence was also perceived to possibly threaten the balance of political power in Michigan. At that time the state was evenly controlled by the Whigs and the Democrats. With the 1852 presidential election a year away, there was already a great deal of interest as to how Strang would instruct his Beaver Island Mormons to vote. In the midst of all this political manuevering, the U.S. District Attorney in Detroit brought charges against Strang and a number of his followers. In May, 1851, the *U.S.S. Michigan* transported the District Attorney to Beaver Island where the suspects came on board. Flimsy charges were levelled but even though the allegations could not be substantiated, Strang and his followers were taken to Detroit, where they were eventually exonerated in a jury trial.

Ironically, the *Michigan* returned to Beaver Island five years later, transporting two men who were involved in a plot to kill Strang. According to an account of the incident published in the *Daily Northern Islander*, the *Michigan* entered St. James Harbor about 1 o'clock on the afternoon of June 16, 1856. About 7 o'clock, Captain McBlair sent word to Strang asking him to come aboard. As he approached, two assassins stepped out from behind a dock building and shot Strang. The assassins then fled on board the *Michigan*. The ship's surgeon was summoned to examine Strang, and he declared that recovery was hopeless. Captain McBlair then refused to turn the assassins over to local officials saying that he would take them to Mackinac and deliver them to authorities there. But when the ship arrived at Mackinac, the assassins were given a hero's welcome.

The *U.S.S. Michigan* then became involved in a scheme of cloak and dagger espionage during the Civil War. A band of Confederate soldiers had an ingenious plan to commandeer the naval war vessel, free Confederate officers imprisoned on Johnson's Island, a Union prison camp in Sandusky Bay, and subsequently use the *Michigan* to raid the port cities along the Great Lakes. The year was 1864, and the primary responsibility of the *Michigan* was to lie at anchor in Lake Erie, guarding those soldiers incarcerated on Johnson's Island. The conspirators were led by Lieutenant John Yates Beall, and to be victorious in their elaborate scheme, the rebels had to overcome two obstacles: first, they needed to distract the officers of the *Michigan* so

Top left, a port view of the *Michigan's* prow which is now on display at Erie, Pennsylvania. Center left, another view of the prow. Center right, the ship's fiddlehead, an ornament that decorated her bow. Below, a photo of the *Michigan* taken in 1868. Photo courtesy U.S. Naval Historical Center.

111

Top right, a drawing of the passenger steamer *Philo Parsons*. Center, the battleship *U.S.S. Michigan* was launched in 1905. Photo courtesy U.S. Naval Historical Center. Right, the new nuclear submarine *Michigan*. Photo courtesy U.S. Navy. Opposite, the passenger steamer *Island Queen*. The two steamers figured in a plot to free Confederate soldiers from a Union prison during the Civil War.

that the vessel could be easily overtaken with little or no opposition; and second, because the *Michigan* was anchored in the lake, they needed another ship from which they could mount their attack.

The first part was easily accomplished. Months earlier, a member of the rebel band had become acquainted with several of the *Michigan's* officers, and had succeeded in gaining their confidence and friendship. According to plan, on the evening of the takeover, this undercover agent would entertain the warship's unwary officers at a party and at some opportune moment he would drug their drinks. Thus incapacitated, the officers would be unable to return to their ship, thereby leaving it vulnerable to the raiders.

The second part of the plot was a bit more complex. To acquire a vessel, the rebels had to virtually become pirates. Selecting his target, Beall quietly boarded the passenger steamer *Philo Parsons* on the first Canadian stop of its normal run between Detroit and Sandusky. At the next Canadian port, a ragged group of nearly 30 men boarded the ship with a heavy trunk. As Beall had anticipated, these men raised no suspicions because the other passengers simply assumed that they were another group of Union deserters who were commonly seen in Canada at that time. As the steamer neared Sandusky Bay, on a signal from Beall the men threw open the trunk, and armed themselves from their portable arsenal. Beall meanwhile had entered the pilot house to take command of the ship. Just as the pirates were congratulating themselves on how smoothly the capture had gone, an unexpected development occurred. Another passenger vessel, the *Island Queen*, had steamed into the bay. Unaware of the situation aboard the *Philo Parsons*, the *Island Queen* innocently drew up to the *Parsons*. With their act of piracy discovered, the confederates quickly transferred all of the passengers and crew from the *Island Queen* to the *Parsons*, and later put them ashore after obtaining a promise of secrecy. The rebels also had taken the *Island Queen* in tow, but she proved to be too cumbersome, and so they scuttled the ship.

The rebels then hastened back to Sandusky Bay, where they nervously waited for the signal to board the *Michigan*. Time dragged on and each passing minute seemed like an eternity. Yet, no signal was forthcoming from the *Michigan*. Believing their plans had gone awry,

Above, the *Michigan* with her sails up. The ship also was equipped with two steam engines which powered her two wooden paddle wheels.

the rebels decided to abort the mission and make their escape. And so under the cover of darkness, the *Philo Parsons* quickly retreated from Sandusky Bay and headed for Detroit, where the steamer was found abandoned the next morning apparently near the spot where the rebels had disembarked to scatter to safety. Their decision was a wise one, for the officers of the *Michigan* had indeed learned of the ambush. They had arrested the rebel spy and had returned to the ship to await the arrival of his accomplices. Had the Confederates carried out their plan, they would have been easily captured.

The last incident occurred in June, 1866. In a bold and brazen effort, a force of more than 1,000 men actually believed that they could take over Canada! Known as the Fenian Raiders, their thoroughly misguided escapade began in Buffalo where they had gathered for the attack. Crossing the Niagara River into Canada, they launched their invasion by capturing the remains of the abandoned and crumbling Fort Erie. Although this force was well armed they quickly were outmatched by the determined Canadian volunteers who had rapidly mobilized to oppose them. When informed that this skirmish was taking place, the United States Navy dispatched the *Michigan* to intercept the vanquished losers as they fled from battle.

The remaining years of the *U.S.S. Michigan's* career were relatively uneventful. She was renamed *U.S.S. Wolverine* in 1905 because a new battleship also had been given the name Michigan. Then in 1912 she

was assigned to the Pennsylvania Naval Militia where she served as a training vessel for the naval reserves. In 1913, she participated in the Battle of Lake Erie Victory Centennial celebrations by having the honor of towing Perry's victory ship the *Niagara* around the lakes. She served as a training ship until August, 1923. On August 12, as she was passing through the Straits of Mackinac, the *U.S.S. Wolverine's* port engine broke a connecting rod. With superficial repairs she was able to return to Erie harbor under her own power. There she remained anchored because complete repairs would be too expensive. Her last captain knew only too well that unless the ship was moved, the *Wolverine* was doomed. She remained at Erie until the end of November, 1928, when the Navy finally decided to have the historic gunboat towed to Put-in-Bay in Lake Erie, site of the Perry Monument. There she remained for the next 20 years, while a group of determined supporters vigorously tried to save her from the scrap yard. But ultimately even the *Wolverine's* dedicated supporters could no longer postpone the inevitable, as this once proud ship was broken up in the spring of 1949. But she did not give up without a fight. On the way to the scrap yard, in seemingly one last display of her strength, she accidentally rammed and sank the launch that was towing her! Then as a lasting testimonial to her greatness, her prow, the front part of the ship, and her anchor were placed on the grounds of the Erie County Historical Society, at Erie, Pennsylvania.   □

Renamed the *U.S.S. Wolverine* in 1905, because a new battleship was given her name, here's the warship at Detroit. Photo by William James Taylor.

THE BATTLE OF LAKE ERIE

"We have met the enemy and they
are ours. Two ships, two brigs,
one schooner and one sloop."

Oliver Hazard Perry

From the very first moment a ship's captain sailed the Great Lakes, he recognized their strategic importance. The lakes had been instrumental to Northwestward movement and development, and many people believed that whoever controlled the lakes would control the Northwest as well. So it was inevitable that war would eventually erupt in the region. The first and only time this issue of supremacy ever became important was during the War of 1812, when the United States openly opposed British aggression toward American merchants and vessels on the high seas. Frequently the British impressed American seamen, seized American goods and confiscated American vessels. While most of the sea battles fought during that war took place on the Eastern Seaboard and the high seas, the Great Lakes region also was a major theater of action. With only these waterways separating British-controlled Canada from the United States, the opposing forces were in frequent contact. While the British had established key military outposts at strategic sites along the northern shores of Lake Erie and the eastern coastlines of Lake St. Clair and Lake Huron, the Americans amassed their defensive batteries along the southern and western shorelines. Aggressive acts between the two sides commenced soon after the Declaration of War on June 18, 1812, with hostile skirmishes and reprisals gradually intensifying, gravitating the local British and American forces toward their ultimate collision, the Battle of Lake Erie.

The most famous and far-reaching naval battle ever to occur on the Great Lakes, the Battle of Lake Erie also was the turning point of the War of 1812 in the entire Great Lakes region. In the early months of the war, the British had firmly asserted their superiority by capturing Mackinac and controlling Detroit. Handicapped by a lack of men and arms, the Americans were unable to either resist or to retaliate with any real strength. Over the course of the next thirteen months, however, the American forces concentrated their efforts toward a build-up of ships and the assembly of troops so that finally prepared and ready to meet their opponent, the Americans were triumphant in gaining supremacy of the Great Lakes once and for all. Their victory, moreover, strengthened the American cause for freedom in this, the second war for independence.

While nearly all of the history books credit Oliver Hazard Perry, the brilliant commander of the American fleet, as being largely responsible for this great naval victory, Daniel Dobbins, a captain of a merchant ship and later munitions-supplier for the squadron, is also deserving of credit, since it was his keen perception that led to the construction of the American fleet in the first place. Anchored at Mackinac on July 17, 1812 when it was overtaken by the British, Dobbins realized that if the United States were to be successful against the British, the Americans would need to establish a lake flotilla of their own. He quickly hastened to Washington where he advised President Madison and his cabinet accordingly. They swiftly approved the plan and appointed Dobbins as a sailing master in the Navy, charging him with the initial responsibility for the acquisition and construction of the vessels. Dobbins retained leadership of the project until Perry's arrival at Erie, Pennsylvania on March 27, 1813.

Gathering a fleet was an almost impossible task, and in retrospect, it is incredible that the battle was ever fought at all, considering the seemingly endless obstacles that confronted Commodore Perry and Commodore Robert Heriat Barclay, Commander of the British fleet. Generally, both sides were hampered by a lack of materials, men, and supplies. The British shortage of manpower was so severe, in fact, that on the day of battle, Barclay was forced to leave one vessel behind simply because he did not even have enough men for a crew.

As for the Americans, their first obstacle was how to obtain the vessels. Since financial restrictions prohibited the purchase of all the warships—Dobbins had been given a meager sum of only $2000 to begin his work—and there wasn't enough time to build all of them either, the Americans relied on good old Yankee ingenuity to muster their naval forces. While the majority of ships were constructed, the *Tigress* and *Somers* were purchased, and the *Caledonia* was captured from the British.

The lack of time and space also dictated that two bases of operation be established. Erie, selected as the main shipyard because of its ideal location and protected harbor, was the home port of six ships: the brigs *Lawrence* and *Niagara,* and the schooner-rigged gunboats *Tigress, Porcupine, Scorpion* and *Ariel.* Black Rock, the secondary base at the northern end of the Niagara River, harbored five other vessels: the brig *Caledonia* and the gunsloops *Somers, Trippe, Ohio,* and *Amelia.* Of these 11 vessels, only nine participated in the famous battle. *Amelia,* judged inadequate by the American officers, was sunk in the harbor at Erie soon after her arrival from Black Rock. Sinking or destroying your own vessels was a common practice because it prevented the ships from falling into enemy hands. *Ohio,* under the command of Captain Dobbins, was absent from the fleet taking on

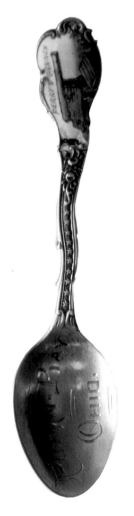

Above, a 1913 commemorative spoon from the centennial celebration of Perry's victory at Lake Erie.

COMMODORE PERRY BREAKS THE BRITISH LINE

fresh supplies at the time of the battle.

Although these bases offered certain advantages, their locations contained inherent disadvantages as well. At Erie, skilled workmen were hard to find as there were no carpenters or boatbuilders among the small village population of less than 500. As a result, Noah Brown, master shipwright of the project, had to import his entire working force from distant cities at great expense and inconvenience. And while the surrounding area provided the necessary timber, other important materials were scarce. So, iron for nails and spikes, canvas for sails, cording for rigging, as well as ammunition and cannons had to be secured from far away Philadelphia, Pittsburg, and Buffalo. Transporting these men and materials proved to be yet another obstacle, for if the long, rugged journey to Erie over poor roads and mountainous terrain challenged the agile horse rider, surely the trek must have seemed nearly insurmountable to the driver of a heavily-laden Conestoga wagon!

Above, a painting of the British flagship *Detroit.* She was built just before the famous battle took place. Courtesy John Robertson collection, the Metropolitan Toronto Library.

121

Above, the *Niagara's* fighting top, and an etching of Oliver Hazard Perry, the young American commodore. Right, a painting of the battle. Courtesy John Robertson collection, the Metropolitan Toronto Library.

The location of Black Rock also was a mixed blessing. Situated at the northeastern end of the Niagara River, the close proximity of Black Rock to the British post at Fort Erie enabled the Americans to attack and seize the *Caledonia,* but it left the port vulnerable to British raids and surveillance even though Black Rock was hidden from immediate view by Squaw Island. Moreover, once the American forces had gathered their ships, another hazard emerged. In order to reach Lake Erie, sailing vessels faced the difficult task of navigating up the Niagara River against a strong five-to-seven knot current. To resolve this dilemma, Perry deployed several teams of oxen on shore to tow the vessels upstream, an awkward and time-consuming procedure that caused a two-week delay in their arrival at Erie.

However, once they were safely assembled inside Erie's harbor, the floating battery was fully rigged, fitted out and armed in rapid succession, so that by the end of July, 1813, all of the vessels were seaworthy and battle-ready at last. Anxious to meet his foe, Perry gave the order to embark for Put-in-Bay, their new headquarters. How proud he must have been as he watched his fledgling flotilla leave the harbor! But their departure was thwarted by yet another obstacle. While the smaller vessels easily crossed the sand bar at the entrance to the lake, the large brigs, *Lawrence* and *Niagara,* identical ships that each drew eight-and-a-half feet of water, could not maneuver the shallow waters that covered the bar. Ironically, the depth of the bar had been considered before the ships were built, but by August 1st when the ships were ready to embark, the water level of the lake had dropped substantially. Faced with this latest crisis,

Perry responded by first attempting to lighten the *Lawrence* by removing all extraneous equipment, including her armament. When this effort failed, Perry consulted with Noah Brown to solve the problem. With expertise and imagination, Brown designed a framework of scows and timbers to give the *Lawrence* sufficient buoyancy to clear the bar. Known as a "camel," a hollow wooden structure approximately 90 feet by 40 feet was affixed to each side of the ship. Water naturally filled the cavities of the camels and when it was pumped out, additional buoyancy was obtained, giving the ship enough room to clear the bar. More than 30 hours later, the *Lawrence* triumphantly floated into Lake Erie and on August 5th the *Niagara*, also aided by Brown's invention, joined the waiting fleet. In full sail, the squadron then easily skimmed the waters westward toward Put-in-Bay.

As difficult as the building of the fleet had been, Perry found that recruiting knowledgeable crew members proved to be an equally difficult chore. Ideally, he needed crewmen who were both able-bodied seamen as well as accomplished marksmen, a rare combination even under normal circumstances. But at that time, locating any crewmen, was a monumental task indeed because most individuals had been already mobilized by the army and were engaged in other action in New York and Ohio as well as on the Eastern seacoast. So by the end of June, 1813, Perry had gathered only 150 men, hardly enough for even a skeleton crew. He then tried to supplement this small force by establishing recruiting stations in the wilderness and although his efforts proved somewhat successful, when the fleet set sail for Put-in-Bay in the beginning of August, the ships were still under-manned. Once again, Perry resolved this latest quandry with the help of General William Henry Harrison, commander of the American troops at Sandusky, Ohio. Harrison's force was preparing to take Detroit and then invade Canada as soon as the British fleet could be defeated. So Harrison dispatched 100 Kentucky sharpshooters who had volunteered to join Perry's crew. This small group of patriots was so loyal to Perry that when they returned home after the war, they influenced their fellow residents to rename their town Hazard, Kentucky, in honor of their beloved commander. These riflemen were

Above, this boarding cutlass was the type used in hand-to-hand combat.

truly representative of those 450 recruits who manned the fleet on the day of the battle. Certainly they were not well-seasoned sailors. For the most part they were adventurous but sincere landlubbers who had to master their own seasickness before they could even think of defeating the British! And master it they did, as during the month of August Perry drilled them intensely and trained them well in the ways of ships and seafights.

As September neared, Perry's forces were getting anxious to put their newly-acquired skills to the test, for they had avoided meeting the British on a number of previous occasions. Although the first two near-encounters were accidental, they were timely reprieves for the Americans, since in both situations the British could have easily defeated them. When Perry was bringing the five vessels from Black Rock, he was not too far from a large squadron of British ships in Lake Erie. But luckily, fog blanketed the area and masked the presence of the Americans, saving them from certain disaster. Later, when Perry was trying to urge the *Lawrence* over the bar at Erie, Barclay and his fleet were hovering in the lake, not ten miles from shore. The Americans were spared once again because the British commander, unable to distinguish clearly from that distance, did not realize just how defenseless the Americans really were. To the contrary Barclay erroneously assumed that the whole American squadron was assembled, and since the British were in no position to take on the entire American fleet, Barclay and his men sailed off swiftly to Amherstburg. The third close encounter occurred during the last week of August, but this time the decision to avoid conflict was the intentional and voluntary choice of Perry, who had sailed to Amherstburg in search of the British. As he neared the British shipyard near Malden, Perry could discern that the large British warship, *Detroit*, was still under construction, but he could also easily distinguish the heavy artillery on shore that protected the British vessels. So he returned to Put-in-Bay to await a more opportune time for their meeting.

Perry didn't have to wait much longer. Three weeks later, early in the morning of September 10th, as the fleet lay quietly at anchor at Put-in-Bay awaiting the day's orders, a lookout spied the entire British fleet approaching from the north. With the ship *Detroit* as his flagship, Barclay was accompanied by the remainder of his forces: the ship *Queen Charlotte*, the schooners *Lady Prevost* and *Chippewa*, the brig *General Hunter*, and the sloop *Little Belt*. The British objective was obvious. With their supplies nearly exhausted, the British hoped to encounter and defeat the Americans, thereby gaining control of the lake and reopening the supply routes the Americans had cut off.

On the deck of his own flagship, the *Lawrence*, named in honor of James Lawrence, commander of the *Chesapeake* who had bravely sacrificed his life in an earlier conflict with the British, Perry hastily began bracing his men and ships for the inevitable clash. Giving a signal to hoist the blue and white battle flag, bearing Lawrence's dying words to his men, "Don't give up the ship," Perry issued the long-awaited command to set sail to meet the British in the lake, where the Americans eventually scuttled their opponents in the most resounding American victory ever to occur on the Great Lakes!

The victory was not an easy one, however. From the start, the British assumed the offensive and maintained it for the greatest part of the battle. Fifteen minutes before noon, with the forces a mile and a half apart, the *Detroit* hurtled the first cannonball toward the *Lawrence,* a shot that luckily fell short of the mark. The *Detroit's* second ball was a direct hit, violently penetrating both bulwarks of the American flagship and fatally injuring one of her crew. When the *Lawrence* opened fire in reply to the British at 11:55, her short guns were incapable of reaching the enemy. So it became imperative that Perry close with *Detroit* as rapidly as possible. Unfortunately, as the *Lawrence* advanced toward the *Detroit,* her 2 long range guns were no match for the *Detroit's* 17 and only the *Scorpion* and *Ariel* were close enough to offer assistance.

By 12:30, she had come within pistol shot of the *Detroit* and the furor of the battle steadily increased, swelling to an earshattering crescendo. For the next two hours, cannons boomed, grapeshot whistled, and men shrieked in agony as they were ruthlessly struck down. Many of the injured ignored their wounds and stalwartly maintained their battle stations, while the more seriously wounded abandoned their posts briefly, just long enough to receive medical attention. Those admirable Kentucky sharpshooters stubbornly held their positions, and from their perches in the rigging, picked off the British one after another. The efforts of these valiant men, proved futile in the long run, however, for they could not save the *Lawrence* from the full might and vengeance of the British fleet. Incredibly, the *Lawrence* withstood the unrelenting assault for two hours, but by 2:30

Left, a 32-pound cannon ball. Above, a look down the muzzle of a cannon.

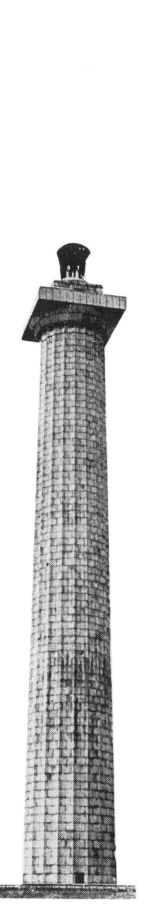

with every one of her guns knocked out of action, it was clear that she could sustain the punishment no longer. Her sails were in shreds, her rigging was shot away, and her rudder was gone. The *Lawrence* was virtually dead in the water. And, of her 103-man crew, 83 had been killed or wounded.

Signalling to the *Niagara*, Perry departed from his once proud flagship, knowing she had served him well. Accompanied by four oarsmen, the American commodore made the hazardous transfer in an exposed rowboat, as grapeshot peppered the skies above and cannonballs churned the waters below. Observing the transfer, the British interpreted the action as a sign of American defeat. This was a lucky mistake for the Americans, for at last the tide of battle had turned! Taking command of the *Niagara* at 2:45, Perry launched his ravaging counter attack. With the *Lady Prevost* and *Chippewa* on his port side and the *Detroit* and *Queen Charlotte* to his starboard, Perry plowed up through the middle of the British line, lambasting all four ships with broadsides. Realizing Perry's strategy, the *Queen Charlotte* attempted to come about so that she could retaliate with fresh starboard cannon. But in the process, she became entangled with the

Detroit and both ships were rendered helpless to the onslaught of the *Niagara*. Once he reached the end of the line, Perry came about and repeated the bombardment, and in less than 20 minutes from when he began to make his run, Perry had at last achieved his victory. The *Queen Charlotte* was first to strike her colors, with the *Detroit* and *Lady Prevost* following soon thereafter. The *Chippewa* and *Little Belt* tried to escape but were halted in the attempt by the *Trippe* and *Scorpion*.

The carnage had been devastating. The dead and wounded were strewn everywhere, and the decks ran red with blood despite the fact that before the battle, sand had been thickly spread to absorb it. When the final body count was made, 27 Americans had been killed and 96 others were wounded, while 41 British were dead and 94 had sustained injuries.

Back aboard the *Lawrence* by 4 p.m., the American leader penned his famous message of victory to General Harrison on shore: "We have met the enemy and they are ours. Two ships, two brigs, one schooner and one sloop." Then, following customary battle procedures, the defeated British officers presented themselves aboard the *Lawrence* to offer their swords in surrender. When they arrived, however, Perry's first genuine concern was of the condition of Barclay who had been severely wounded in battle. Perry broke with tradition even further, for he refused to accept their swords, thereby acknowledging their dignity as human beings and fellow officers. The following day, both British and American forces participated in a touching, joint ceremony to bury their dead.

Assessing the battle, both sides had been fairly evenly matched. While the American vessels outnumbered the British ships nine to six, three of the British ships, the *Queen Charlotte, General Hunter,* and *Lady Prevost,* had been in service for several years, giving them the

Opposite, the Perry Monument at Put-in-Bay on South Bass Island in Lake Erie. Courtesy Dossin Great Lakes Museum Collection. Above left, the jacket which Perry wore during the battle. From The "Niagara" Keepsake, Perry's Victory Centennial Souvenir Series. Left, Perry hoisted this battle flag to inspire his men to victory.

Above, a replica of a carronade, a short range gun used on the *Niagara* which fired either round shot or grape shot.

advantage over the infant American ships which were all virtually new vessels. Then too, the British ships carried more guns—63 to 54—and the British were equipped with many more long range guns, making them more effective from a distance. In terms of manpower, both forces were again comparable, even though a headcount reveals that 532 men were aboard the American ships while there were only 440 on the British vessels. On the day of the battle, however, some 80 Americans, ill with the flu, were unfit for duty and did not participate. Then of the two opposing commanders, Robert Heriat Barclay was undoubtedly the more experienced commodore, since he had served well under Lord Nelson at Trafalgar eight years before. Barclay, too, was acutely aware of the serious consequences of combat, for he had lost his left arm in that famous battle. While young Perry had not been so personally involved in war, he was aptly qualified nonetheless. Having led a squadron on the East Coast, Perry had diligently worked his way up through the ranks and what he lacked in firsthand knowledge, he more than compensated for in resourcefulness and strategy.

With so many things being equal, two factors played a significant role in the American victory. The first, a tactical manuever, was an accident, but an opportune one, nevertheless. When Perry's observer spotted the British ships at 10 a.m., Perry had already formulated his battle plan. His most advantageous approach was to pit his largest vessels against the largest British vessels so that the *Lawrence* and *Niagara* would challenge the *Detroit* and *Queen Charlotte* respectively, the *Caledonia* would take on the *General Hunter*, and the rest of his fleet would offer general support to the larger American ships and hold off the remainder of the British as well. While Perry's plan was a good one, he never got the chance to use it because as the British fleet approached, their battle line was different from what Perry had expected. Consequently, the *Niagara* was forced to change her position in order to challenge the *Queen Charlotte*. However, the *Niagara*

The *Niagara* only carried two cannons. Above, a replica of an 18-pounder that had the range of nearly one mile.

remained distant during the heaviest part of the battle and used her two long range guns from afar, rather than closing in to attack her opponent. This proved to be a mixed blessing. Because the *Niagara* failed to divert the attention of the second largest British ship, the *Queen Charlotte* was then able to join in on the assault of the *Lawrence*, causing its annihilation. Ironically, the *Niagara's* failure to enjoin the enemy ship could not have been more effective if it had been intentionally calculated. While the *Lawrence* was totally incapacitated, the British vessels also were in shambles and now the *Niagara* became Perry's ace in the hole, providing him with an unused battleship ready to defeat the British at a time when all of their vessels were nearly destroyed.

The second major factor contributing to the American victory was Commodore Perry himself. Well-loved as a commander, Oliver Hazard Perry had justifiably earned the absolute respect and loyalty of his men. That he was able to frequently inspire his troops to expend almost superhuman effort to defeat their enemy, it is easy to understand why his men held great admiration for him. Clearly he was brave and clever, but he was also chivalrous and compassionate, continuously revealing his genuine concern for others. Even with the British in view, Perry, realizing his men would miss their noon meal, ordered it served early so they would be more comfortable in battle. Perry's concern for the enemy likewise illustrated his unselfishness. When Perry and his men had returned to Erie, his men were jubilant; but Perry cautioned them not to disturb the injured Barclay with their celebrations.

But whatever the reasons, Perry's conquest held great significance for the Great Lakes region for when Perry won Lake Erie, he cleared the way for General Harrison to pursue the British into Canada, beating them back to the Thames River where the Americans once again completely routed their adversary in the Battle of the Thames in November. War continued in other areas until both the United

States and England agreed on a settlement and jointly signed the Treaty of Ghent in Belgium on Christmas Eve, 1814, which returned all captured territories and forts to their original countries. Detroit and Windsor, too, quickly reestablished harmonious relationships and representatives from both cities participated in a Peace Banquet in March, 1815.

One hundred years later, Americans still remembered Perry's glorious victory, and appropriately commemorated the event. The *Niagara* was resurrected from the sandy bottom of Erie harbor where she had been sunk nearly 80 years before to preserve her. After she had been fully restored, she was towed proudly by the *Wolverine* on tour of the Great Lakes region. From Buffalo to Chicago, thousands were privileged to view this famous brig. Her journey ended at Put-in-Bay on the centennial anniversary of the victory and a week-long celebration of ceremonies and banquets followed. Today she rests quietly at Erie, a silent reminder of our glorious past. ☐

Right, a bow view of the restored *Niagara*. She is on display at State Street, in Erie, Pennsylania. After the first restoration of the ship in 1913, she participated in the centennial celebration of the battle by touring the lakes. She was towed by the *U.S.S. Wolverine.*

Top left, the ship as she appeared on the starboard side, looking forward before restoration efforts began in 1913. Center left, just prior to her launch after being restored. Both photos from The "Niagara" Keepsake, Perry's Victory Centennial Souvenir Series. Left, the *Niagara* was restored again in 1950. Photo by John Guba.

ROGER BLOUGH

A great ship asks deep waters.

George Herbert
"Jacula Prudentum"

The schooners which sailed the Great Lakes during the 19th Century made a significant contribution to the economic development of the region. Transportation on land through the wilderness was difficult until the second half of the century, so much of the early expansion was dependent on the commercial shipping industry. But while these grand sailing ships were instrumental to the advancement of commerce, their usefulness to the merchant was limited for two reasons. First, because of restrictions on their structure and design, many of the vessels had reached a maximum size for sailing efficiently. Consequently, they could hold only a certain amount of cargo which in turn meant the tradesman could earn only so much profit from each voyage. Secondly, because sailing vessels were dependent upon the wind for propulsion, their schedules were often erratic and unpredictable. Inevitably, shopkeepers were unable to plan accurately and precisely for the distribution of their goods at terminal ports. To the merchants this loss of time meant a loss of income. So out of economic necessity, all of the major shipbuilders concentrated their efforts on making the necessary technological improvements to resolve these very difficulties. The first obstacle dealing with the limit on the size and capacity of a ship was overcome by their experimentation with a variety of materials for hull construction—iron and steel rather than wood—that enabled them to build longer vessels that still remained strong and seaworthy. The second problem of how to maintain a consistent sailing speed was solved by the use of the steam engine. Ships that were powered by an engine were no longer subject to the whims of nature and could establish fixed schedules. And eventually the big, new steamers made the old sailing vessels obsolete as commercial carriers. But it is ironic that in view of today's high fuel costs and uncertainty over continued sources of supply, sailing vessels may yet prove to be an economically feasible alternative for the American merchant marine industry, and may be sailing the Great Lakes and the high seas once more.

Nonetheless, steam navigation arrived in the Great Lakes in 1818. Named the *Walk-in-the-Water*, this 330-ton steamer was also rigged with sails—her builders apparently not having complete faith in her new fangled engine. A passenger ship, she sank in 1821, but the salvage crew was able to save her engine, and they placed it in a new vessel named *Superior*. More steamships, without sails, arrived in the years that followed, most of them providing passenger service from the East.

Then in 1861, the first iron-hulled merchant vessel was registered in the United States. A propeller ship, she was given the appropriate name *Merchant*. Stretching a length of 190 feet, she also claimed a beam of 29 feet, and boasted a hull depth of 14 feet. Eight years later, another significant event in the history of today's commercial sailing fleet took place as the *R. J. Hackett,* the first bulk carrier to sail on the Great Lakes was launched at Cleveland. Her length measured 211 feet, and while she was made of wood, the *Hackett* is also noteworthy because of her unique design. With her navigational quarters forward, her engines aft, and her hold and hatches in between, she thus established that special profile that would eventually set apart the bulk carriers of the Great Lakes from ships on all other waters of the world. But the dimensions of these ships were meager indeed when measured against those of the ore carriers built during the first decade of this century. Incredibly, in merely 50 years, commercial transports had more than tripled their lengths, doubled their beams, and more than doubled their hull depths. For while many of the 75 registered vessels in 1907 were some 400 to 500 feet long, 14 of those freighters, for example, stretched to 600 feet. Their widths had also expanded to nearly 60 feet, and their hull depths were enlarged to 32 feet. But even those ships are small when matched against the giants of 800 feet and more which sail the lakes today.

Throughout this century, however, of all the great commercial sailing fleets to dominate the shipping lanes of the Great Lakes, one fleet has overshadowed all others. This fleet, owned by the United States Steel Corporation, is the largest American fleet and over the years, its ships have always had the reputation of being the highest caliber. U.S. Steel's quest for excellence, in fact, has become a long standing tradition, and the company has continuously worked to upgrade its fleet, outfitting its ships with the latest advancements in construction and technology.

Frequently their experimentation and research has been beneficial to the entire merchant marine industry. For example, U.S. Steel led the way in establishing a winter shipping season on the Great Lakes. Normally, once winter had arrived and heavy ice had set in the lakes, all vessels either returned to shipyards for repairs or put in at port until the spring thaw reopened the shipping lanes. All lake traffic was virtually halted because if the freighters became ice-bound, they were unable to free themselves. Because idle ships and lost time add

Taconite pellets, the usual cargo for the *Roger Blough.* The freighter can carry 45,000 tons of this high grade material.

ROGER BLOUGH

This photo clearly shows the *Blough's* five segmented holds. Photo by John Chidester.

up to a loss of income, U.S. Steel set out to resolve this dilemma. They conceived a freighter, equipped with sophisticated instrumentation to aid navigation and to improve communications, so that the ship would be able to continuously receive all relevant information about any changes in the ice conditions on the lakes and thereby avoid the perilous ice floes wherever and whenever possible. They imagined a solid ship, with tremendous horsepower and a double plated bow, so that it would be able to cut through five inches of ice. They dreamed of a mighty ship that winter could not stop. They envisioned the *Roger Blough.*

In October, 1967, U.S. Steel proudly revealed its plans for this new flag ship. Named in honor of their former Chairman of the Board, the M/V (motor-vessel) *Roger Blough* was, at the time she was built, the largest vessel ever totally constructed by Great Lakes shipbuilders. With a completion date of July, 1971, U.S. Steel had commissioned the American Shipbuilding Company to build their new freighter at the firm's shipyard in Lorain, Ohio. Work progressed according to

Her starboard bow covered with ice, the *Roger Blough* is one of a few ships to work the winter shipping season.

schedule and the ship was nearly finished when tragedy struck. On June 24, 1971, just one month prior to her anticipated launching date, a disastrous fire erupted in the stern section of the freighter. Four members of the construction crew perished in the blaze and the engines were extensively damaged. Thus her first voyage was delayed nearly a year while her engines were replaced and other minor repairs were made. Finally, on June 13, 1972, under the command of Captain J.N. Rolfson who had also supervised her trial runs, the *Roger Blough* embarked on her maiden voyage.

When she was launched, this super-sized transport ushered in a new generation of oversized lakers. With a length of 858 feet, a width of 105 feet, and a depth of 41 feet, 6 inches, her colossal proportions overwhelmed the awe-filled spectators who had gathered for the event. And it's interesting to note that her length actually surpasses the height of the U.S. Steel corporate headquarters building in Pittsburgh. The *Roger Blough* also contains two diesel engines that provide her with enough power to reach a maximum speed of 16.5

A view looking forward from the aft section of the starboard deck. The *Blough* measures 858 feet in length.

139

Above, Captain Neil Rolfson, former master of the *Roger Blough.* Right, her starboard bow. Photo by Paul Lydy. Below, a drawing of the *Blough* which compares her length to that of a 200-foot freighter of the 19th Century.

miles per hour when she is fully loaded. Capable of bearing 45,000 tons of cargo in her five segmented holds, she is equipped with a self-unloading apparatus that efficiently ejects her cargo at the rate of 10,000 tons per hour. In fact, as a result of this amazing efficiency, she is the only Great Lakes vessel to consistently load cargo on one side of the ship, then shift to another dock, where additional cargo will be loaded on the other side.

Though the *Roger Blough* was fundamentally engineered to be an ore carrier, she also was designed to provide maximum comfort for her officers and crew. In fact, most of the ship's facilities are intended to create an atmosphere that is as homey as possible. Ample state-rooms with private baths, for example, are assigned to all men: single cabins both forward and aft are reserved for the officers, while rooms in the stern are each shared by two crew members. All quarters are nicely furnished and the occupants can regulate both the heating and cooling systems to their personal satisfaction. Dining rooms and galleys, equipped with toasters, griddles, coffee-makers and refrigerators, are always available for a quick midnight snack or a late evening lunch. Recreation rooms provide the crew with a friendly place to relax, watch television, or play cards. And laundry rooms fitted with washers, dryers, and irons help to make the more mundane chores of living a little bit easier.

The same attention to comfort and convenience that is found in the private quarters also is present in both the design of the pilot house and the operational machinery of the ship. Situated in the upper reaches of the bow, the glass enclosed bridge provides an unobstructed, panoramic view of the water. And the latest equipment has been installed to help simplify the operation of the vessel. Remote controls manipulate the engines, a bow thruster enables the ship to move sideways, and a controllable pitch propeller keeps the ship properly balanced, compensating for changes in the load or for rough sea conditions. This propeller also can reverse the vessel's direction without reversing the engines.

According to her former skipper, Captain Rolfson, the *Blough* has another unusual trait when she is traveling in rough seas. A common characteristic of the smaller 600 foot freighters is a particular type of motion which is commonly referred to as "springing." This movement of the hull of the vessel can actually be seen as the ship moves through the rough seas. When the *Roger Blough* is working in heavy seas, however, a distinctive wave like motion can be readily seen traveling down the length of her deck as the hull actually undulates in this manner. She doesn't spring up and down at all.

This wave like motion may seem quite appalling to many people. Imagine yourself standing aboard the *Blough* in a good blow watching her deck heave and bend so that the ship actually arches her back! In the early days of shipbuilding, ship designers attempted to counteract this force by building a very rigid hull. This was accomplished by the construction of two arch supports which stretched nearly the full length of the ship. In today's construction techniques a vessel is made

During the author's trip on the *Roger Blough* a very unusual incident occurred. As a result of the malfunction of an oil strainer, the starboard crankshaft was fractured. A crankshaft change was necessary, but rather than bring the ship in for repairs, the *Blough* kept operating on one engine at two-thirds normal speed while the crew and service personnel dismantled the affected engine. (The work is shown above.) The ship did go into the shipyard for a total of four days while cranes removed and replaced the crankshaft, although the *Blough* went back to work operating on a single engine while the other was being repaired. The ship ran on one engine for six weeks, It was the first time this type of operation had been accomplished.

When she was constructed in 1971, the *Roger Blough* was the largest vessel ever totally manufactured by Great Lakes shipbuilders. Photo by Paul Lydy.

to heave and bend and this flexing action is built right into the design of the ship. I was once told by an officer aboard an aircraft carrier that the deck may bend as much as four feet in a very rough sea.

Restricted to the larger ports because of her immense size, the *Roger Blough* loads her usual cargo of taconite pellets at Two Harbors, Minnesota in the upper westward reaches of Lake Superior and disperses it for further processing to the southernmost shores of Lake Michigan at South Chicago, Illinois and Gary, Indiana. Then, returning north, taking her eastern lake route, and carrying the same cargo, she travels through the Straits of Mackinac and proceeds down the length of Lake Huron to the southeastern banks of Lake Erie where she unloads the rest of those pellets at Conneaut, Ohio. Conceivably, a single passage might encompass more than 850 miles.

Despite the harshness of the winter season, the *Roger Blough* covers the expansive Great Lakes territory usually unhampered by the icy conditions. The first to succeed at making this passage, she alone was able to plow through the frigid waters for the duration of the 1975 winter shipping season. An obvious asset to U.S. Steel's fleet, the imposing *Roger Blough* has satisfactorily fulfilled the expectations of her owners and has justifiably earned the respect and admiration that is rightfully hers alone. ☐

Top left, this view of her stern shows the unloading beam. Center photo by Steve Whittlesey. Left, at the controls on the bridge, that's Walter Boone, the *Blough's* Second Mate when this photo was taken in 1978.

CARL D. BRADLEY

The ship teetered on the crests,
She wallowed in the troughs,
She groaned, she moaned with stress and strain,
Every fibre of her body was wracked with pain.

Richard A. Belford
"The Chiefs of Bygone Days"

Hailed as the largest ship of her day on the Great Lakes, hull number 797, the *Carl D. Bradley,* was built by the American Shipbuilding Company of Lorain, Ohio, in 1927. Her very first cargo established a record for the lakes when on July 28, 1927, she carried 14,627 gross tons of limestone to Buffington, Indiana. Having the most modern navigational aids and termed the "ultimate" in freighter construction, she measured 638 feet, 9 inches in length, had a beam of 65 feet, 2 inches, a depth of 33 feet, and measured 77 feet from the top of her pilot house to her keel. Her self-unloading boom was 160 feet long. Fitted with a turbo-electric power plant which generated 5000 shaft horsepower, she could manage approximately 14 miles per hour when fully loaded.

The *Bradley* had already enjoyed a satisfactory career, when in April, 1958, the employees of the Bradley Transportation Company, Michigan Limestone Division of the U.S. Steel Corporation, received the top award from the National Safety Council for having operated more than three-and-a-half years without a lost-time injury, which, by the way, established a new world safety record for the marine transportation industry. In fact, the *Bradley* had undergone 18 drydock "sight and survey" inspections in her 31 years, 12 more than the six required for that time.

By fall of 1958, although she had been in service for 31 years, as ships go, the *Bradley* was relatively young. Yet her owners decided she needed a new cargo hold which they planned to install come the winter lay up. Then, at Cedarville, Michigan in October of that year, she had struck the bottom and had ruptured one of her plates. Although this minor damage was repaired, other repairs also were badly needed. In fact, her entire crew was well aware that several of her bulkheads were so badly rusted that you could see from one compartment to another, and that her ballast tanks leaked to the point where the pumps had to be used quite often.

A month later, on November 17, one of those mean fall storms was kicking up on Lake Michigan as the *Bradley* discharged her cargo of limestone at Gary, Indiana and headed for Manitowoc, Wisconsin at 9:30 p.m. Having covered 27,000 miles that season she was headed for winter lay up which meant that her crew would be going home for the season, a welcome thought indeed. However those thoughts of loved ones and comfort were soon dismissed when the ship's captain received orders to return to Port Calcite, Rogers City, Michigan for another load of limestone.

Captain Roland Bryan, age 52, of Collinwood, Ontario had been the skipper of the *Bradley* since 1954. He also had served another 17 years as mate and seven years as master in the Bradley fleet. Bryan was a bachelor, and one of that breed of sailors who would dare to challenge the mighty fresh water hazards that could be found in the fury of those Great Lakes November storms. But with storm warnings posted and a severe southwest wind lashing the seas into a powerful force, perhaps Captain Bryan now reflected on his concern for the condition of his ship. It had been on his mind for some time, and he had even shared his feelings in a letter that he had written earlier to Mrs. Florence Herd, of Port Huron, Michigan, in which he wrote: "This boat is getting pretty ripe for too much weather. I'll be glad when they get her fixed up."

Undoubtedly, those thoughts once again occurred to Captain Bryan as he guided his ship north in Lake Michigan under the protection of the Wisconsin shore. Smaller ships had already scurried to safe ports as the *Bradley*, carrying 9000 tons of water ballast, rode the storm well throughout the night. By first light on Tuesday, although gale warnings were still up, everything seemed normal and the *Bradley* continued her northern route. After all, she had been in countless other storms before and while the weather wasn't getting any better, the immense size of the ship seemed to dispel any immediate thoughts of danger.

By afternoon, having altered her course slightly to the northeast, the *Bradley* now had a direct following sea. The winds, still raging from the southwest had increased to 60 miles per hour, and had built the waves to some 20 feet with intermittent ones reaching a height of 30 feet. It must have been an awesome sight. Actually, very few photographs have ever documented a ship working in tremendous seas. And the term "working" is a most accurate description. Ships are built to withstand the stress and torture that such gigantic waves produce, and the heaving and twisting of a ship under these rough conditions can actually be observed by those on board.

The *Bradley* was holding her own as she neared the top of Lake Michigan. The Beaver Island chain lay just off her starboard bow. Dinner was being served and in just a few more hours they would be out of the rough weather and safe in the shelter provided by the islands. At 5:26, First Mate Elmer Fleming acknowledged a routine message from the dispatcher at Calcite which was passed through by Central Radio and Telegraph. There was no mention of any problem.

The watch worn by Frank Mays during his 15-hour ordeal awaiting rescue in Lake Michigan.

CARL D. BRADLEY

Twenty-three-year-old Deck watchman Frank Mays had finished his supper and was beginning his duties in the tunnel. During unloading operations the deck and holds are strewn with fine bits of stone that are later washed down with water, and Mays was in the process of pumping off the accumulated water. After completing this job, he was proceeding forward to the dunnage room where miscellaneous equipment was kept, when he heard a loud thud. Mays knew something had happened, but gave it no further thought until moments later when another thud was heard.

Suddenly there was a tremendous bang! The sound had a definite ring of danger. Peering aft from the bridge, in the obvious direction of the noise, Captain Bryan and Fleming could hardly believe their eyes. The *Bradley's* rear section was sagging! Captain Bryan ordered engine stopped, rang the general alarm, and ordered Fleming to send a distress call. Fleming shouted his desperate message: "Mayday... Mayday...Mayday...This is the *Carl D. Bradley*...We are breaking in two and sinking...Our position—approximately 12 miles southwest of Gull Island...Any ships in the area please come to our aid...."

According to Frank Mays, "the aft section sagged so badly, that you had to look hard to see it, for the ship was humped about eight feet amidship."

Fleming continued to repeat his terse message and all receiving radio operators now listening intently must have been horrified to hear Captain Bryan in the background, yelling to the crew "Grab lifeboats! Get the jackets!" Bryan then signaled seven short and one long blast of the ship's whistle to order "abandon ship."

Those last few moments aboard the *Bradley* were a nightmare. Members of the crew rudely awakened by the abandon ship alarm had little time to grasp the impact of the situation. Mays frantically ran below for his watch and wallet, and Fleming, realizing that he was without a lifejacket, rushed to his quarters to get one.

When both men returned to the bridge, the deck was arched like a

Above, a starboard broadside view of the ship. Photo courtesy M. J. Brown collection. Right, the *Bradley* heads through the Soo Locks at Sault Ste. Marie, Michigan. Below, the steamer unloads near the Blue Water Bridge at Port Huron, Michigan. Both bottom photos courtesy Manitowoc Maritime Museum collection.

writing snake, and with the booming clash of metal smacking against metal, the aft section broke away from the rest of the ship just behind the unloading boom on the starboard side. The final blow had been dealt, the *Bradley* was broken in two, and with the snapping blue sparkle of severed electrical wiring, all radio contact was lost.

Attempting to pull themselves hand over hand along the rail on the high side of the forward section which was rolling madly, Captain Bryan and a few others inched their way to the bow of the ship while others tried desperately to free the liferaft. Seconds later, without warning, the *Bradley* lurched to port and flung those men clinging to the forward end into the icy waters.

Fighting to stay on the surface, with the frigid water literally taking his breath away, Mays saw that he was within an arms length of the raft and grabbed it. He could hear, but he could not see many of the others who were crying out for help. Fleming, also thrown from the forward section, tried desperately to grasp at anything nearby. Sloshing about in mountainous waves, he heard someone yelling to him. It was Mays. Fleming managed to get to the raft and as both men struggled to get aboard, the forward section of the *Bradley* sank.

Peering through the storm, both men now attempted to locate the others. Barely discernable above the roar of the waves, faint cries were heard. Men were screaming "Over here," and through the gloomy darkness Fleming made out a figure of a man whom he recognized as Deck watchman Gary Strezlecki. After a desperate struggle to aid their shipmate, and still maintain a hold on the raft, they finally pulled him aboard.

Soon another cry was heard—more of a groan at first—then louder and closer, almost next to the raft. Overjoyed at finding another mate, and yelling encouragement to each other, they pulled the man aboard. It was Dennis Meredith who had been asleep in his bunk when the general alarm had sounded. He was wearing only light clothing, and had no shoes, and he had turned blue from the cold. Now in the eerie glow from the water lights on the ring buoys, other shipmates flashed in and out of sight between the giant waves. Although only a few moments had actually transpired in the tragic ordeal, it already seemed like hours. Each man on the raft was in agony at the thought of what had just happened. It was almost too much to bear. But fighting back their emotions, each of the four men continued to call out in search of their mates.

Fleming knew that his distress calls had gotten through and that it was simply a matter of time before they would be rescued. As that thought rushed through his mind, Fleming fought the pitching raft to find the signal flares. The storm seemed to be getting worse, but miraculously he found the survival kit and in total darkness launched several flares.

Then in an immense spectacle, looming high in the darkness, the aft section of the *Bradley* rose some 200 feet in the air and began its final plunge with its cabin lights still on. As the forward end of the cabins touched the water, the sky was illuminated with a bright

The *Bradley* as she passes under the Ambassador Bridge at Detroit. Photo by William James Taylor.

orange glow that was quickly followed by an ear-splitting explosion as the water hit the boilers. It was 5:30 p.m., Tuesday, November 18, 1958, and the *Carl D. Bradley,* one of the giants of the Great Lakes, was gone.

As the four men clutched the rolling eight-foot raft, they continued to shout to the others. Although at times it seemed that the other voices were very close to them, monstrous waves obscured their view. Then, deep inside each man, those fearful questions of what had actually happened kept turning in their minds. Where were the others? What happened to Bryan? Did the men below deck get out? With each chilling wash of the waves, they knew the gravity of the situation, but they also knew that in order to survive, they must keep going—stay alert—and not give up.

Fleming's Mayday calls had gotten through and the rescue teams were already responding. The closest vessel to the scene was the German freighter, *Christian Sartori,* and the master, Captain Paul Mueller, who had been monitoring the distress calls, advised that he would proceed at once to the scene, only four miles away. In normal conditions, this distance could have been covered in minutes, but with the storm now at its peak, it took the *Sartori* two hours.

Although those flares from the survivors were spotted from

A view of the *Bradley* unloading cargo from the port side. Photo courtesy M. J. Brown collection.

aboard the *Sartori*, and in spite of the fact that Captain Mueller had driven his ship unmercifully into the teeth of the gale, upon his arrival to the location where the *Bradley* was reportedly last heard from, he found nothing in the water but a raincoat and a tank. Making a thorough search of the area and finding no survivors, at 7:00 p.m., he reluctantly radioed his initial search report: "I believe all hands are lost. No lifeboats are visible."

Anxiously awaiting any word from the disaster area, families of the stricken *Bradley* crew began a vigil of hope that lasted through the night. Out of the *Bradley's* crew of 35 men, 25 of them were from Rogers City, and only four lived outside of Michigan. Two men, George Sobeck, Jr. and Sylvester Sobeck did not sail on the *Bradley* this last time. They had been given leave to attend the funeral of George Sobeck's father.

At 10:40 p.m., the 180-foot Coast Guard Cutter *Sundew* arrived on the scene to begin its search, and at 2:30 a.m., the Coast Guard Cutter *Hollyhock* out of Sturgeon Bay, Wisconsin joined the group.

Through the night, while the four survivors fought the cold and the fury of the storm on their unprotected raft, the search continued. Fleming and Mays fought off the temptation to sleep by forcing themselves to talk, count, sing, anything to keep their minds active.

Top right, a port topside view of the *Carl D. Bradley.* Center, an up-close look at the ship's unloading apparatus. Photos courtesy Manitowoc Maritime Museum collection. Right, a lifeboat from the ship. Courtesy Great Lakes Historical Society collection.

Three times their raft was simply picked up and thrown end over end in the raging seas. During one of these violent episodes, while they fought to regain their hold of the raft, Strezlecki and Meredith were lost. The temperature was dropping and ice was forming in their hair as the storm finally seemed to be letting up. Fleming had saved one last flare in hopes of having a good chance to attract a vessel should one come near. But their hopes were crushed as the *Christian Sartori* practically brushed their raft as it made one of her passes and the single flare that was left failed to ignite.

To also assist in what had now become the largest rescue attempt in Great Lakes history, three Coast Guard helicopters from Traverse City, an Albatross search plane from Selfridge Air Force Base, and a Navy PV2 from Glenview Naval Air Station, along with the steamers *Elton Hoyt* and *Robert C. Stanley* joined the search.

It was 8:55 a.m., November 19th, when the first confirmed report of survivors was heard. The *Sundew* had picked up Frank Mays and Elmer Fleming from the raft, between High and Gull Islands, approximately 20 miles from where the *Bradley* had gone down.

The search for other survivors continued during the daylight hours of November 20th and 21st. And Coast Guard rescue aircraft continued making a daily air search of the area for several days after that.

In addition to the two survivors, Fleming and Mays, only 18 other bodies were ever found. In the spring of 1959, the Army Corps of Engineers verified the position, size and shape of the hulk believed to be that of the *Bradley*. Sonar equipment aboard the survey boat *M.S. Williams* confirmed that the *Bradley* was lying in some 360 to 370 feet of water 53.25 miles northwest of Boulder Reef.

Later, another search conducted by the Global Marine Exploration Company of Los Angeles, appeared to dispute the findings of the Coast Guard Marine Board of Investigation which found that the *Bradley* had broken in two before sinking. Through the use of an underwater television system, the motor vessel *Submarex* established "that the sunken steamer as it lies, apparently has continuity of the lower cross section of her hull structure confirming earlier sonar findings that the vessel lay in one piece."

Frank Mays, now the lone survivor of the *Carl D. Bradley* disaster, states "I will never change my story. I saw the *Bradley* break in half. I saw two distinct pieces of her hull. I saw the severed electrical wiring flash when it broke in half, and I saw two separate pieces of the hull go down."

The final episode of one of the most tragic and chilling chapters in Great Lakes history came to an end in 1960, when the litigation surrounding the *Bradley* disaster was finally resolved with a $1,250,000 settlement that was paid to the 35 claimants who had originally sued for a total of $16,490,000.

There is one final footnote, however. Elmer Fleming, former First Mate on the *Carl D. Bradley,* died in 1970. Thus Frank Mays is the only survivor of that devastating 15-hour ordeal in the chilling waters of Lake Michigan in November, 1958. ☐

EDMUND FITZGERALD

Our deck was a welter of seething foam.
Great frothing tops mounted our rails
and smothered the hatches with
liquid hillocks of roaring whiteness.

Richard A. Belford
"The Storm"

Thousands of interested spectators were filled with awe as the largest freighter yet to have been conceived on the Great Lakes was launched on June 7, 1958, at the Great Lakes Engineering Works at River Rouge, Michigan. Mrs. Edmund Fitzgerald, wife of the Chairman of the Northwestern Mutual Life Insurance Company, the firm for which the ship had been built, smashed the traditional champagne bottle over the bow of the 729-foot *Edmund Fitzgerald,* named for her husband. Probably the largest collection of pleasure boats, tugs, and freighters ever assembled for such an event also were on hand to offer a grand salute to this magnificent newcomer, and her smooth launching was reportedly "perfect" in every way. Perfect, except for the death of one of the onlookers, a man by the name of Jennings Frazier of Toledo, Ohio, who died suddenly at the scene, stricken with a heart attack.

If the *Fitzgerald* were still around today, however, this incident would probably have been completely forgotten, but since the ship and her 29 crewmembers were inexplainably lost in a storm on Lake Superior, November 10, 1975, it gives credence to those superstitions that were first nourished in ship-building communities long ago—if an unlucky or unfortunate incident occurs during the launch of a vessel, it is a bad omen, and the ship itself is considered to be extremely unlucky. But one could hardly tell if the "Big Fitz" was an unlucky ship during her 17 years of active record breaking service. The 75-foot beam super carrier was chartered to the Oglebay-Norton Company and her distinctive, massive appearance projected an image of strength and longevity. She also was "the" favorite vessel of ship-watchers and marine photographers along her busy route.

Her appointments were superb. Tiled baths, deep-piled carpeting and special furnishings from the J.L. Hudson Company in Detroit, contributed just the right finishing touch to her tastefully decorated and plush quarters. The record cargoes which the *Fitzgerald* carried

This broken oar from the *Fitzgerald* was found on the shore of Lake Superior at Whitefish Point, Michigan, by Mason Hall of Gladwin and William Peterson of Oscoda.

were even more impressive than her unique appearance. At the close of the shipping season in December, 1968, it marked the seventh season that the *Fitzgerald* had carried more tonnage through the Soo Locks than had any other ship in a single year. On July 25th of that year, she also carried 30,260 net tons of taconite pellets in a single load to become the first vessel in history to pass through the Soo Locks with that much cargo. Then in September, the following year, she carried a cargo of 30,690 net tons, breaking her own record.

But her size and performance were not the only things that made her special. When Captain Peter Pulcer was in command, he would occasionally "serenade" the sleeping tourists along the banks of the St. Mary's River at the Soo by piping music through the ship's public address system. And while passing through the locks, he would frequently come out on the observation deck with his bull horn and offer the tourists interesting facts about his ship.

The *Fitzgerald* continued to bask in her record breaking glory without a single incident of misfortune or calamity and in June, 1969, her owners received an award for having completed eight accident-free years. Although she never lost her popularity, the *Fitzgerald* was soon out of the record breaking picture, however, as newer and even larger ore carriers came into being.

Then on November 9, 1975, the first, and last tragic episode of the *Edmund Fitzgerald* began to unfold. Captain Ernest R. McSorley, a veteran with 44 years of sailing experience was in command as the *Fitzgerald* departed the Duluth-Superior harbor at 1:15 p.m. with 25,116 tons of taconite pellets in her hold. The weather was unseasonably mild. Warm temperatures and calm seas seemed to lure all of the crew members out on deck, to relax, bask in the sun, and enjoy one last beautiful fall day. It was a routine trip for Captain McSorley, and certainly a "piece of cake" for the "Big Fitz" considering her previous record hauls.

These pleasant conditions soon changed, however, as an immense low pressure system over Escanaba, Michigan began moving to the north-northwest across Lake Superior at 7:00 a.m. on the 10th. As this weather front moved through, the entire eastern half of the lake began showing it's teeth. This monster system that some say equaled the 1913 storm of storms, churned the seas into a vicious animal.

By afternoon, Captain McSorley had radioed Captain Jesse Cooper, aboard the *Arthur M. Anderson* approximately eight miles astern, that he had lost two vent covers and some railings, that he was taking water, and that the *Fitzgerald* had developed a list—she was leaning to one side. Requesting that the *Anderson* keep her in sight, McSorley asked for a fix on his position as the *Fitzgerald's* radar also had become inoperative.

Snow squalls and the eventual arrival of darkness made it difficult for the *Anderson* to continue its observation of the *Fitzgerald*, but at 7:10 p.m., with the *Fitzgerald* still appearing on his radar screen, Captain Cooper radioed Captain McSorely to find out how he was doing. In a quiet tone, Captain McSorely answered, "We are holding

EDMUND FITZGERALD

A starboard bow topside view of the *Edmund Fitzgerald.* Photo by J. Maynard.

The *Fitzgerald* was "the" favorite vessel of shipwatchers along her busy route. Photo courtesy M. J. Brown collection.

our own." Yet about this same time the *Fitzgerald* had contacted the Swedish ship *Avorfors* which was anchored in Whitefish Bay to inquire whether the light and the direction finder at Whitefish Point were in operation. Captain Woodard, the pilot aboard the *Avorfors* replied that both were inoperative because of a battery power failure, and according to Woodard, Captain McSorley sounded worried because he commented, "The Fitzgerald is in a big sea—I've never seen anything like it in my life."

Those reportedly were the last words to ever come from the captain or crew of the *Fitzgerald.* She was approximately 15 miles west of Whitefish Point, and she was caught in the midst of 27-foot to 30-foot waves, hurricane winds, and a menacing, following sea.

At 7:25 p.m., after the *Anderson* had safely cleared its way through a heavy snow squall, Captain Cooper shockingly discovered that the *Fitzgerald* had disappeared from his radar scope. He tried to reach her by radio, but there was no response. Sailing into the area where the "Fitz" should have been, Captain Cooper searched for her through the darkness, but he knew that the *Fitzgerald* had sunk and he immediately contacted the Coast Guard saying, "The Fitz is gone."

Search efforts by all of the ships in the area began immediately, and these vessels were later joined by aircraft, but no survivors were

The career of the "Fitz" lasted only 17 years, but she set many new records. Photo courtesy M. J. Brown collection.

ever found. Enough floating wreckage and debris was recovered, however, to substantiate the fact that the *Fitzgerald* had gone down. That she had vanished so quickly, it was as though some supernatural force had literally plucked her from the lake. Estimates have been made which state the *Fitzgerald* sank within 12 seconds. Thus her crew never had a chance to launch a liferaft, to put on a lifejacket, or even to send a Mayday call!

While the U.S. Coast Guard Marine Board of Investigation completed an exhaustive study of the disaster including an examination of numerous close up photographs taken by CURV 3, a cable controlled underwater recovery vehicle, the Coast Guard could not establish with certainty the direct cause of the wreck. Their report, however, did state that ineffective hatch covers were the best and probable reason for the disaster.

Some people believe in the theory that the *Fitzgerald* sustained major damage after striking the shoals near Caribou Island some three hours before she sank. Others say she actually broke in half while being caught between the crests of two giant waves. It is this author's opinion that during the tremendous storm, the *Fitzgerald* lost one or more of her hatch covers, and was simply overwhelmed by those giant waves which were not even encountered by the other ships in

A drawing by the author of how the *Fitzgerald* might have looked in a heavy snow squall. Above right, a drawing of the sunken ship aft from the pilot house and deck. Right, a forward view of the bow. Both drawings courtesy U.S. Coast Guard Marine Board of Investigation Report.

the area. Thus she was forced into a submarine-type dive that took her down in less than 12 seconds. Photographs from the investigation show that the window casing of the pilot house was bent inward, suggesting such a nose dive. In addition, if the *Fitzgerald* had broken in two on the surface, it would seem likely that there would have been enough time for the radio operator to send at least one distress call. But if she had gone down in almost a straight dive, those on the bridge would have been instantly smashed to the rear of the pilot house by the tons of water that was pouring in. In this situation, each man would have been rendered totally helpless, unable to hold even a telephone.

The controversy over what actually happened to the *Fitzgerald* was further enhanced on September 24, 1980 when two crew members from the Jacques Cousteau research vessel *Calypso,* spent 30 minutes filming the wreck from a two-man submarine at a depth of 529 feet. Discounting the Coast Guard theory, Jean Michel Cousteau speculated that the *Fitzgerald* broke in two while on the stormy surface of Lake Superior. Stating that they found "the bow section extremely dented," Cousteau said that "something had to bang against it." He further stated that despite the fact that there were no calls for help, it was his opinion that the freighter did not sink quickly. "Had the ship

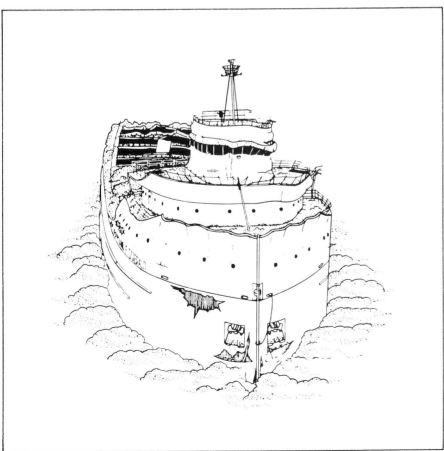

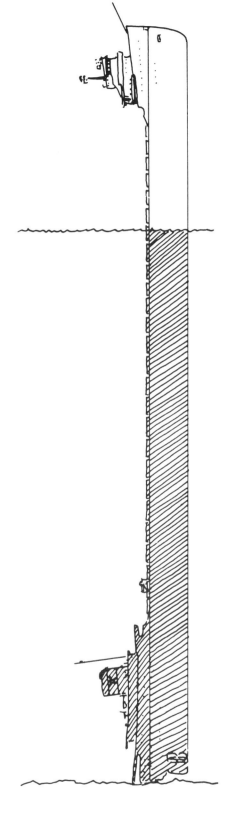

Because the *Fitzgerald* was 729 feet long, and she sank in 529 feet of water, it is incredible to imagine that if she were stood on end, the ship would reach 200 feet above the water.

Above, this U. S. Coast Guard photo shows that the pilot house window was pushed inward, supporting the theory that the ship went down in a submarine like nose dive. Above right, another U. S. Coast Guard photo of the bridge. That's the telephone cord at the left side of the picture. Right, this drawing shows the approximate position of the *Fitzgerald* as she lies on the bottom. Courtesy U. S. Coast Guard Marine Board of Investigation Report.

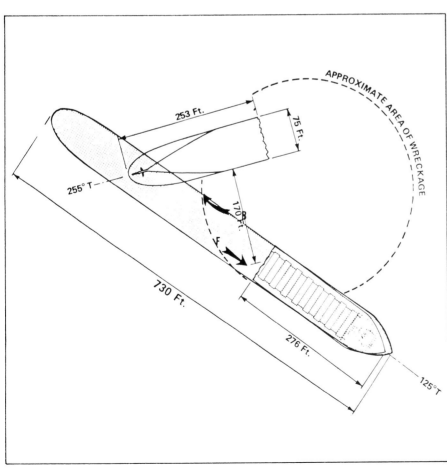

broken in two pieces and instantly sunk, the bow would have been further from the aft section," Cousteau said, explaining that the two sections were found 150 feet apart. But this theory also appears to contain a contradiction. For if the broken sections of the hull are this close together, then it would seem more likely that she broke in two when she hit the bottom, because had the hull broken in two on the surface, in sinking to the bottom, it seems logical that the two sections would have drifted away from each other and therefore would be a greater distance apart.

Whatever the reason for the disaster, the intimate relationship that we share with the *Edmund Fitzgerald* will long continue, because she really was a special ship. Perhaps you can remember catching sight of her in the last hours of some golden sunset, recalling how it seemed that she was passing by just for you. And if you looked close enough, the Captain was waving...just for you. □

Below, a model of the *Edmund Fitzgerald* as she lies on the bottom of Lake Superior. The model was made by Bruce Bigger. Bottom, a photo of the *Arthur M. Anderson* She was the closest ship to the *Fitzgerald* when the tragedy occurred. Photo courtesy Dossin Great Lakes Museum collection.

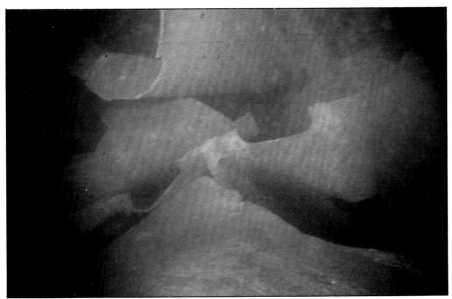

Top left, one of 13 liferings found from the *Fitzgerald*. Courtesy Great Lakes Historical Society collection. Center left, this U. S. Coast Guard photo shows some of the twisted metal from her hull. Left, the *Fitzgerald* will long be remembered as one of the finest ore freighters to ever travel the Great Lakes. Photo by Garnet W. Lozon.

CLIFFS VICTORY

They took a worthy victory ship
And began a giant's chore.
They cut her in two and added a snip,
So's to haul more Great Lakes ore.

As the long, sleek freighter plies the waters southbound on the St. Clair River, connecting Lake Huron with Lake St. Clair, she emits a low, resounding whistle that acknowledges her northbound counterpart. Unwittingly, she also mesmerizes the admiring crowd on shore, enchanting them with the echo of the promise she symbolizes. Deep within their thoughts, they can hear the hypnotic, rhythmic splash of waves breaking insistently over the bow of a ship in open waters; they can feel the steady, refreshing spray-filled breezes blowing persistently across the lake; and they can see the inspirational, graceful seagulls soaring and diving overhead in an age-old ritual. Indeed, the call of the sea is irresistible, although to most of those enthusiasts who now line the riverbanks, they can answer only with their imaginations. For them, the excitement and danger of lurching and rolling in heavy seas, or the romance of skimming lightly over the surface of glassy, moonlit waters is possible only by pretending that they are aboard one of those massive ships that now pass before them.

In recent years the crowds who have come to picnic on the grassy knolls alongside those heavily traveled shipping lanes have increased in number as casual observers and armchair sailors alike pursue their favorite pastime of shipwatching. While some are content to simply enjoy the random passing of ships, others, who must be infected with some type of sea fever, try to make their seafaring dreams more real by religiously consulting the newspapers for the vessel passage schedules, or by intently peering through binoculars for the first glimpse of the ships on the horizon. Many of this latter group are obsessed with their hobby. These serious, and often extremely knowledgeable shipwatchers will frequently consult a personal library of fleet recognition books at the arrival of each new ship, or they will carefully catalogue and photograph them in much the same way that birdwatchers will record their observations. Fellow shipwatchers will often compare notes and exchange information, sometimes even seeking to trade or sell nautical memorabilia. Many devotees, in fact, possess extensive collections that may include ships' wheels, whistles and fleet line flags, unique and often highly priced artifacts that were obtained by scavenging through shipyards or by knowing the right collector.

The urge to personally communicate with these passing ships is almost uncontrollable, and even the most indifferent landlubber finds it difficult to resist waving to the hardy seamen aboard the decks of the freighters. To the enthusiastic shipwatcher, however, a single wave is not enough. They come down to the piers armed with flare guns, bullhorns or megaphones to try and coax a salute from the skipper. Some of the more enterprising individuals may actually track down the names and addresses of the crewmen or captains, and will correspond with them regularly to learn more about life aboard their favorite vessels.

It is of such stuff that dreams are made, and so it is no wonder that one of the biggest charmers and a favorite lady of all shipwatchers is the *Cliffs Victory*. Her striking appearance at once commands the attention of all who patiently wait for her to pass by. With a vivid green and black color scheme, a flared bow, the unusual location of her hatches, and the great length aft of her smokestack, she is a proud sight indeed. She projects an image of powerful determination and silent strength as she glides almost effortlessly over the water to carry out her mission of transporting a huge cargo of iron ore from the western mining ports of the upper lakes region to the steel mills along the southern shores of the lakes.

Originally named *Notre Dame Victory*, she was built in Portland, Oregon in 1945 and was designed as a salt water vessel. Purchased by the Cleveland Cliffs Iron Company from the U.S. Marine Administration in 1951, she thus became the first ocean-going vessel ever to be converted to a Great Lakes ore carrier, a monumental accomplishment indeed.

The Cleveland Cliffs Iron Company, an Ohio-based firm, had at that time been successfully working the productive mines of the Upper Peninsula, and had been traveling the waterways of the Great Lakes with commercial metals for nearly 100 years. But when the demand for iron ore rose sharply in the early 1950s, the company realized that it needed to expand its shipping fleet. With its future flagship, the *Edward B. Greene* already under construction, company officials decided that yet another bulk freighter was badly needed. Unfortunately, when they submitted their order for this ship, they discovered that all construction berths were occupied. Thus building a new vessel was out of the question. Their only alternative was to buy a ship, and the company immediately began a search to find one. Interestingly enough, they discovered that ocean-going vessels could, in fact, be adapted for use on the Great Lakes. So wasting no time in the arduous and challenging task that lay ahead, they selected the *Notre Dame Victory* because she was the best ship available, and

The starboard bow anchor of the bulk freighter *Cliffs Victory*.

CLIFFS VICTORY

moreover, her double reinforced bow would be an asset in the conversion process, and it would also give her the maximum support she needed for her responsibilities which lay ahead.

From her berth in the St. James River near Newport, Virginia, the *Notre Dame Victory* was towed to the Baltimore shipyard where, in just 90 days, her extensive conversion was accomplished. Almost unbelievably, the mammoth 455-foot vessel had been split apart and a 165-foot midsection had been added. This procedure would again be performed in 1957, when she would be lengthened another 96 feet, 3 inches. But on March 21, 1951, she was christened *Cliffs Victory*, and the occasion was truly a victory for her owners.

By no means was the *Victory's* transition from an ocean-going vessel to a Great Lakes vessel finished, however, because she now faced a new obstacle—a difficult 3,000 mile journey that would take the ship through the Gulf of Mexico and up through the breadth of the United States via the Mississippi River, through the Illinois Waterway System, and the Chicago Sanitary and Ship Canal to Lake Michigan. Her final destination was the American Shipbuilding

A converted ocean-going vessel, two sections totalling more than 261 feet have been added to the *Victory* to make her a suitable Great Lakes ore carrier. Photo by Paul Lydy.

Company shipyards at Chicago, where she would be finally fitted out for service as a bulk carrier.

Amazingly, not one segment of her long trek was completed under her own power—she was forced to rely on tugs to tow her the entire distance! Frequently manned by just a skeleton crew, she sometimes carried as few as 20 men on board to oversee her progress on the long trip northward. Hazards lurked around every bend. While low-lying bridges and other aerial structures loomed menacingly overhead, treacherous rocks often lurked beneath the surface. Additionally, she would have to pass through nine different locks on her voyage. Clearing the numerous bridges (one allowed her only five inches of room to spare) was a simple chore compared to her final challenge. To clear the last lock, she needed a miracle because her 620-foot length was 20 feet longer than the lock itself. As her apprehensive crew looked on nervously, the ship slowly progressed through the narrow passageway. Then, almost unbelievably, the lock operators opened both of the lock gates at the same time! Carefully the front gates were opened allowing tons of Lake Michigan water to surge in. The rigid tow lines snapped as the force of the water drove the *Victory* backwards. Gradually she regained her momentum over this immense surge of water, and she was cautiously inched forward just enough to enable the rear gates of the lock to be closed. Then with the expertise of a Swiss watchmaker, she was delicately guided through the lock, without further incident, and the *Victory* floated victoriously into Lake Michigan.

Once completed, *Cliffs Victory* was ready for a triumphant maiden voyage as a Great Lakes ore carrier. On June 4, 1951, she headed for Marquette to take on her first load of iron ore. It was the beginning of a very productive career on the inland seas that has endured for three decades. The fastest ship on the lakes when she was launched, the *Victory* could easily attain speeds of up to 20.5 miles per hour and

Opposite, a view of the *Victory's* port stern. Left, a port broadside view of the ship. Courtesy M. J. Brown collection. Below, the port bow of the *Victory* in dry dock. Note the bow thrusters at the bottom of the photo. Courtesy Lewis Langell collection.

CLIFFS VICTORY

THE CLEVELAND-CLIFFS STEAMSHIP CO

The fastest ship on the lakes when she was launched in 1951, the Victory can attain a speed of 20.5 miles per hour. Photo by Paul Lydy.

she would often complete her long distance voyages literally days ahead of the competition.

Interestingly, at the start of her career, she was not well liked by her masters. Skippers were skeptical to take her out, fearing that her flared bow would inhibit docking procedures or that it would obstruct their view of the docks. They also were leery of her speed, because her prop was considered to be too large for a ship of her size. To some extent their misgivings were justified as it was frequently said that a good, steady hand was needed to keep the lively lady in check. There would be no sleeping at the wheel of the *Victory*.

Her unique characteristics, however proved to be an asset. On one occasion, a fierce storm had swept across upper Lake Huron in 1951. While most vessels in the vicinity had stopped to wait out the blow, the *Victory* was not deterred by the weather. Braving the elements, she proved her prowess by plunging on through the storm, unloading her cargo on time at Conneaut, Ohio. On her return trip upbound, as she reached Port Huron, her crew noted that those less adventurous ships who had chosen to safely wait out the storm were just beginning to come in off the lake. That skeptical attitude concerning her design was now completely forgotten, because it was that flared bow and lean configuration that had enabled her to slice through the

Above left, a starboard view of the pilot house. Left, her first skippers did not like her flared bow, believing that it would inhibit docking procedures.

179

pounding storm! This valiant ship would never be questioned again.

Life aboard ship for the crew of the *Victory* is similar to that found on the other ore carriers. While the daily work schedule may vary according to the particular needs of the vessel, the bulk of the duty takes place during daylight hours. When in port, once the day's work is complete, members of the crew are free to go on liberty or "up the street" as it is referred to on the lakes. On board ship, the officers have private quarters while the crew members are paired up two in a room. And they have most of the comforts of "home" as the ship is well equipped with the necessary appliances for carefree living.

"Here comes *Cliffs Victory!*" is the shout of the devoted ship-watchers along the shore. From their enthusiastic greeting, it is

evident that their statement is much more than a casual observation. It is a heartfelt compliment, a fervant tribute to a gallant ship, a ship that has earned and maintained a flawless reputation on the lakes for over a quarter of a century. They gaze at their idol with awe, and yet with a deep sense of melancholy too, because the faded leaves are now blowing airily across the park. Sadly they realize that soon heavy ice floes will clog the waterways and the *Cliffs Victory* will be gone from view for another long, cold winter. Undeniably, they will miss her. But as the first signs of spring break through the last traces of winter, those loyal shipwatchers will resume their stations along the waterfront to scan intently for the season's first sighting of their favorite lady! ☐

Here are two views of the *Cliffs Victory* coming and going, taken from the Blue Water Bridge at Port Huron, Michigan.

Epilogue

Are we seeing the last views of the era of the elegant ship? I think so. The small work vessels in the early days of navigation on the Great Lakes had a positive beauty which soon transformed into the larger, graceful schooners. With the advent of steam power, the development of lakes vessels took a giant step. The small passenger and cargo ships, noble in appearance, soon were dwarfed by their majestic successors. As iron and steel hulls came into being, the race for size was on, but the vessels produced were splendid excursion boats and distinctively magnificent cargo ships.

As the demand for larger cargo ships accelerated to the need for today's super-lakers, the demise of the grandiose passenger vessels had already taken place. And now, during this transition from the traditional freighter to the giant carriers, the last glimpses of the elegant ships are passing before us.

Many attempts to bring back even a tiny part of excursion boating have all been in vain. The last few remnants of passenger boats appear to be dying. Even the call for the restoration of these historic vessels have gone unanswered. No one has the money or the interest to fund the return of a grand old girl.

And so, with a 1000-footer now easily doing the work of three predecessors, and the talk of even 1500-footers coming, the ship-watchers view them as one might look at an enormous drab building, rather than to admire a beautiful lady.

J. Clary

Bibliography

Angelo, Frank. *Yesterday's Michigan.* Miami, Florida: E.A. Seeman Publishing, Inc., 1975.

Bald, Clever F. *Michigan In Four Centuries.* New York, New York: Harper & Row, Publishers, 1961.

_____. *Perry Transfers To The Niagara.* U.S.A.: Michigan Bell Telephone Co., 1964.

Ballert, Albert G. *"Enter Roger Blough!"* TELESCOPE, September-October, 1972.

Battenfeld, Esther Rice. *"Hail And Farewell, Lovely Lady Of The Lakes."* INLAND SEAS, 1967, No. 4, 267-276.

Belford, Richard A. *The Ragged Rimes Of A Great Lakes Steamboat Man.* Cleveland, Ohio: Richard A. Belford, Publisher, 1974.

"Bob-Lo: Anchors Aweigh (But Call First)." The Detroit *News.* June 16, 1978.

"Bob-Lo Bolts Signs Of Spring Into Place." Detroit *Free Press.* April 3, 1978.

Bowen, Dana Thomas. *Memories Of The Lakes.* Cleveland, Ohio: Freshwater Press, Inc., 1969.

_____. *Lore Of The Lakes.* Cleveland, Ohio: Freshwater Press, Inc., 1969.

Bugbee, Gordon P. *"The D-III: Grandest Ship Of The Lakes."* TELESCOPE, February, 1965.

_____. *"The David Dows."* TELESCOPE, August, 1959.

Chrysler, Don. *The Story Of Grand River,* Grand Rapids, Michigan: 1975.

Clark, Dr. James A. *"The Edmund Fitzgerald."* TELESCOPE, January-February, 1976.

"Commerce Club Revives Story Of Greatest Lake Schooner." The Toledo *Blade,* March 16, 1915.

"Crack Lake Passenger Ship Burns In Drydock." Port Huron *Times Herald,* September 9, 1924.

Dobbins, Captain W.W. *History Of The Battle of Lake Erie (September 10, 1813) and Reminiscences of the Flagships Lawrence and Niagara,* Erie, Pennsylvania, Ashby Publishing Co., 1876.

Douty, J.F. *The Conversion Of An Ocean Cargo Vessel To A Great Lakes Ore Carrier And Associated Delivery Problems.* New York, New York, The Society of Naval Architects and Marine Engineers, 1952.

Duncan, Francis. *"The Story Of The D & C."* INLAND SEAS, 1951, No. 4, 219-228.

Ellis, William Donohue. *Land Of The Inland Seas: The Historic And*

Beautiful Great Lakes Country. New York, New York: American West Publishing Company, 1974.

England, Captain R.W. *"Save The Wolverine."* Notes of INLAND SEAS, 1945, No. 1, 36.

"First Iron-Clad Warship Wins A Reprieve Till Oct. 1." The Port Huron *Times Herald.* August 29, 1948.

"Fitzgerald Broke In Two On Surface—Calypso." The Detroit *Free Press,* September 26, 1980.

Fitzpatrick, Doyle C. *The King Strang Story.* Lansing, Michigan: National Heritage, 1970.

Frohman, Charles E. *Put-In-Bay.* Columbus, Ohio: The Ohio Historical Society, 1971.

——————————. *Rebels On Lake Erie.* Columbus, Ohio: The Ohio Historical Society, 1965.

"Great Lakes Calendar: October, 1953." INLAND SEAS, 1953, No. 4, 293.

"Great Lakes And Seaway News." TELESCOPE, May—June 1975.

Hardy, George E. *"The David Dows."* INLAND SEAS, 1945, No. 3, 54.

Hatcher, Harlan and Erich A. Walter. *A Pictorial History Of The Great Lakes.* New York, New York: Bonanza Books, 1963.

Havinghurst, Walter. *The Long Ships Passing.* New York, New York: The McMillan Co., 1957.

"Highlights And Sidelights Of The Battle Of Lake Erie." Erie, Pennsylvania: Holiday Inn, n.d.

Hilton, George W. *The Night Boat.* Berkeley, California: Howell-North Books, 1968.

History Of The Great Lakes, Vol. 1. Chicago, Illinois: J.H. Beers & Co., 1899; reprinted, Cleveland, Ohio: Freshwater Press, Inc., 1972.

"Icebreaker Bringing Blough Here." The Lorain *Journal,* January, 19, 1977.

Kirkwood, Ernest. *"From Salt To Fresh Water—Or, The Story Of Cliffs Victory"* INLAND SEAS, 1960, No. 3, 203-205.

La Vriha, Jack. *"Blough Set To Battle Lake Ice To Lorain."* The Lorain *Journal,* February 3, 1977.

Leidy, Mrs. Paul Allen. Interview by James Clary, February 21, 1973.

Lochbiler, Don. *Detroit's Coming Of Age, 1873 to 1973.* Detroit, Michigan: Wayne State University Press, 1973.

Lovette, Lieutenant Commander Leland P. *Naval Customs Traditions And Usage,* United States Naval Institute: Annapolis, Maryland, 1939.

Mastics, Al. *"The War That Won the Peace"* in commerative booklet of Inter-Lakes Yachting Association: *The Sesquicentennial Of The War That Won The Peace 1813-1963.* Vermilion, Ohio: Great Lakes Historical Museum, 1963.

Miller, John F. *"The David Dows."* TELESCOPE, March, 1961.

Mills, James C. *Our Inland Seas.* Chicago: A.C. McClurg & Co., 1910; reprinted, Cleveland, Ohio: Freshwater Press, Inc., 1976.

M.V. Roger Blough. USS Visual Services.

O'Brien, Michael J. *"Tashmoo."* TELESCOPE, October, 1965.

"Origin Of Put-In-Bay." INLAND SEAS, 1947, No. 3, 195-196.

"Passenger Boats At Sandusky, 1880-1947." INLAND SEAS, 1956, No. 3, 219-220.

Patton, Mike. "Ore Freighter Awaits Icebreaker." The Port Huron Times Herald, January, 1977.

Perry's Victory Centennial Souvenir: The Niagara Keepsake. New York, New York: The Journal of American History, 1913.

Ratigan, William. Great Lakes Shipwrecks & Survivals, Grand Rapids, Michigan: Wm. B. Eerdmans Publishing Company, 1971.

Reed, J.E. Perry And His Flagship The Niagara. Erie, Pennsylvania: Erie County Historical Society, 1950.

Reves, Haviland F., "The Bob-Lo Boats—A Living Tradition." INLAND SEAS, 1957, No. 3., 184-197.

Rolfson, Captain Neil. Interview by James Clary, June 26, 1978.

Rosenberg, Max. The Building Of Perry's Fleet On Lake Erie. Harrisburg, Pennsylvania: Pennsylvania Historical and Museum Commission, 1950.

Rozynek, Joseph F. Interview by Mrs. Irene McCreery, September 20, 1971. Toledo Public Library, Toledo, Ohio.

Schellig, Robert I., Jr. "Legal Lore: The Grand Experiment." TELESCOPE, March-April, 1975.

"The David Dows." Toledo Blade, May 17, 1881.

"The Last Port." Edited by the Perry Flagship Fund, Erie, Pennsylvania, n.d.

The Sesquicentennial Of The War That Won The Peace 1813-1963, Inter-Lake Yachting Association, Ohio, 1963.

"She's The Queen." Toledo Blade, April 21, 1881.

Spencer, Herbert Reynolds. U.S.S. Michigan, U.S.S. Wolverine. Erie, Pennsylvania: A-K-D Printing Co., 1966.

"Steamer South American." THE MARINE REVIEW, September, 1914.

"Stretching The Lake Season—Michigan Challenge," GREAT LAKES SHIPPING, April, 1975.

"Swept By Icy Gales." Chicago Tribune, November 30, 1889.

This Fabulous Century: Sixty Years Of American Life. New York, New York: Time-Life Books, 1969.

"12 Lake Ships Are Missing Or Ashore In Gale." The Detroit Free Press, December 9, 1927.

U.S. Department of Commerce. Bureau of the Census, Tenth Census of the United States, 1880: Special Reports, Vol. 2, "Shipbuilding Industry of the United States, 1884," by Henry Hall.

Weber, Dan M. "Cruising Down The River." INLAND SEAS, 1955, No. 4., 295-296.

_____. "The Last Of The Sidewheelers." INLAND SEAS, 1957, No. 1, 5-9.

Wellejus, Ed. "Erie Maritime Museum Boosted." The Erie Times, February 5, 1975.

Woolson, Allen M. "Confederates On Lake Erie." U.S. Naval Institute Proceedings, April, 1973.

Worden, William M. "The Battle Of Lake Erie, September 10, 1813." TELESCOPE, September, 1963.

Index